Ballet

This book is dedicated to
Dame Marie Rambert, DBE, ('Mim')
to whom I owe so much.

Robert Harrold

Ballet

BLANDFORD PRESS

Poole   Dorset

First published in the U.K. in 1980

Copyright © 1980 Blandford Press Ltd,
Link House, West Street,
Poole, Dorset, BH15 1LL

British Library Cataloguing in Publication Data

Harrold, Robert
  Ballet (Blandford colour series).
  1. Ballet
  I. Title
  792.8   GV1787

ISBN 0 7137 1006 3 (Hardback edition)
ISBN 0 7137 1099 3 (Paperback edition)

Phototypeset in Monophoto Apollo
by Oliver Burridge and Co. Ltd.

Printed in Hong Kong by South China Printing Co.

Contents

Acknowledgements

The author would like to thank the following people for their help in the preparation of this book:

. David Poole, Artistic Director, CAPAB; Valerie Logan; The Royal Winnipeg Ballet; Tokyo Ballet Theatre; Mary Clarke, Editor, *The Dancing Times*; Mary Moresco; Australian Information Services; John Travis, Archivist, London Festival Ballet; The Royal Danish Ballet; Harry Goss; David Palmer, The Australian Ballet.

Colour photographs have been reproduced by kind permission of the following:

Victoria and Albert Museum, Crown Copyright: plates 1, 21
Reg Wilson, London: plates 2, 4, 8, 9, 11–13, 15, 16, 20, 22–26, 29–43, 45, 46, 48–52, 55, 56, 58–60, 62
The Scottish Ballet: plates 3, 5, 6, 17, 18, 53, 57
Barry Gray/National Ballet of Canada: plates 7, 44
Martha Swope/National Ballet of Canada: plates 10, 19
Martha Swope, New York: plates 14, 61
CAPAB: plates 27, 28
Herbert Migdoll, New York: plate 47
The Australian Ballet: plate 54
Anthony Crickmay, London: plate 63
Simon Rae-Scott/The Royal Ballet School: plate 64

Black and white photographs have been reproduced by permission of: Snowdon/Camera Press, London (Frontispiece); The Trustees of the Wallace Collection (page 14); The Mansell Collection (pages 26, 28, 135); John Travis, London Festival Ballet (pages 30, 32, 37, 41, 43); Nederlands Dans Theater (page 110); Barry Gray/National Ballet of Canada (page 114); Simon Rae-Scott/The Royal Ballet School (page 128).

Introduction

Ballet has surely never been so popular as it is today. National or State subsidised companies may be found in countries as far apart as the USSR, South America, USA, New Zealand, China and Canada. Companies may be small or large, but all are presenting the art of ballet to a responsive public. Ballet has no language barriers and can be understood and enjoyed by all; it is a truly international art.

Why is ballet so universally popular? In times of stress or violence there is an instinctive reaction towards the arts. In ballet the purity of the classical line, the blending of music and movement and the visual impact of colour, costume and scenery, all combine to give great harmony and satisfaction, offsetting the harsh realities of modern living.

The great increase in public interest in ballet in recent years is largely the result of films and television, which have enabled millions to see the great companies and dancers of the world. In other media too, ballet has made its mark. Dancers receive excellent coverage in magazines and newspapers, and ballet personalities can vie with pop stars or film figures. Ballet has never before had such a large following.

Encouraged by this publicity, thousands of children now learn the art of ballet and examiners from the Royal Academy of Dancing and the Imperial Society of Teachers of Dancing in London, travel the world assessing the potential of students. Ballet techniques are also used in many training routines outside pure dance. In the field of sport, Olympic gymnasts and skaters use ballet in their training. John Curry, the former world ice skating champion, takes a ballet lesson every day and his company presents works which incorporate a blend of ballet and skating. In the medical field ballet techniques are also used to strengthen limbs and muscles and to develop co-ordination.

A book on ballet must present something of the background of its subject. A student recently commented that the beginnings of ballet were so boring, 'all that about Louis XIV, Beauchamp and Noverre . . . I always go off to sleep'. Nevertheless, just a comment on the nineteenth-century romantic ballet and the development of the classical technique

7

would be a very incomplete picture. The gradual growth of ballet and the influences encountered throughout its history all contribute to its form and meaning today. To some this may seem dull, but it is, after all, a dancer's heritage.

Teachers, ballet masters and choreographers of the past have all added to the creation of this great art: Pavlova inspired Helpmann and Ashton; Diaghilev gave Western Europe a true vision of Russian ballet; Nijinsky restored the importance of the male dancer; Taglioni established the role of the ballerina; and Genée presented and maintained a standard of ballet in the music hall.

The 1948 film, *The Red Shoes* was a great box office success and inspired many to take up dancing. Lynn Seymour, the ballerina, director and choreographer, came to ballet after seeing this film. It is difficult to assess the numerous performances and companies which have led others into the ballet field; the attraction of ballet as a career remains strong.

Ballet is a flexible art form and allows for changes in its evolution. New musicians and choreographers continue to present challenges to the world of dance, such as Ashton's *Jazz Calendar* and MacMillan's *Elite Syncopations*, both of which revealed strong contemporary influences and were enormously successful on the ballet stage. Nevertheless, the classic ballets continue to hold their popularity, in the same way as the plays of Shakespeare or the music of Mozart.

Because of the great interest being shown in modern dance, a section on the subject has been included in this book. This may serve as a brief introduction to a technique that has proved a strong influence on present day ballet.

This book can only act as an outline to the art of ballet: how and where it began, its development, how a dancer trains and a mention of famous companies, dancers, choreographers and ballets. Its size precludes much that should be mentioned, but for those who wish to know more, a list of books for further reading has been added. To help readers new to ballet, and consequently unfamiliar with the terms used in this book, a comprehensive glossary is included which, it is hoped, will serve as a mini-dictionary.

8

1
The Beginnings of Ballet

The beginnings of dance stem from the beginnings of creation itself and many beliefs and legends tell of the creation of the world as the dance of God. It is therefore not surprising that dance is found in practically all cultures and is regarded as the indispensable art form from which all others are derived. The Roman poet Lucius wrote, 'The dance is the richest gift of the Muses to Man'. Early man danced to celebrate birth, death, joy, marriage and the seasons of the year. He also danced in imitation of the animals that he hunted.

Gradually dance changed with the development of the various civilisations and cultures and a fixed pattern of steps and movement became established. Each civilisation had its own individual dances. These were divided into two forms, those that were danced on special occasions with a ritual background and those that were performed by professionals and entertainers. This is a division that has come down through the ages and is found today in our ballroom and theatre dancing.

With the passing of each century and the decline and fall of nations, each new civilisation brought fresh approaches and ideas. Tracing the beginnings of dance and the development of ballet can be compared to assembling a jigsaw puzzle. Each period of time has added another piece, building up the pattern of ballet today.

When Europe emerged from the Dark Ages, dance was in a simple form and generally performed out-of-doors in circles or chain formations, e.g. the Farandole. Fra Angelico, the fifteenth-century artist, shows angels in paradise performing this dance in his painting of the Last Judgement. The spiral patterns which the dancers make can be found incorporated into various works of art and architectural designs, and many centuries later this dance was to appear in the great Russian classical ballet, *The Sleeping Beauty*.

It was in Italy, during the Renaissance, that the next development in dance began. This was one of the most important periods in history, producing some of the greatest painters, musicians and sculptors ever known and a wonderful enrichment in the arts in general. Dancers at

9

this time, together with other artists, turned towards the ideals of ancient Greece for their inspiration, and movement developed a flowing quality, the use of the foot and instep giving a rise and fall to the body. The top of the body was turned with a contrary movement known as *Maniera*, which is now referred to in classical ballet as *épaulement*, and the dancers began to use the space around them to form harmonious and balanced patterns. In many of the great paintings of the period, such as those by Leonardo da Vinci (1425–1519), these qualities were very much in evidence.

Italy, during the Renaissance, was divided into many states ruled by the great families of the time: the Medicis of Florence, the d'Estes of Ferrara and the Viscontis of Milan. Each of these families employed their own dancing master (the teaching of dancing was entirely by men; women as teachers did not appear until many centuries later) and dance was an art that the nobility learned as a matter of course, through which they gained an understanding and appreciation of related subjects. One of the great dancing masters of this time was Domenica of Ferrara (?–1462) who created dances of great beauty. He emphasised qualities which he considered essential for good dancing. Unhappily these are not followed by teachers today.

A popular form of entertainment was the masquerade which was usually performed during a dinner or banquet. In Italy these elaborate and extravagant performances became known as 'dinner ballets' and were to have a great influence on the court entertainments of the rest of Europe. With each course dancers would appear, representing mythological characters associated with the dish that was being served. Neptune, with Tritons, would herald the arrival of the fish; Jason, in search of the Golden Fleece, would come with the lamb; and the fruit course was linked with the goddess Pomona. New ideas and novelties were constantly sought for these ballets and there was a great rivalry between families, each vying with the other to out-do the spectacle and grandeur of their rivals. It was from these court entertainments, with their visual appeal, that the beginnings of ballet emerged.

In France the ballets were known as court ballets or *ballets de cour* and one of the most famous was presented in Paris in 1581. It was devised by Catherine de Medici, the dowager queen of France, a very powerful and politically minded woman. Her Italian dancing master, Balthazar de Beaujoyeux (?–1587), produced the ballet which blended dance, song, speech and spectacle in a performance that lasted from ten at night until three the next morning. Machines were used to effect transformations and enabled performers to descend from above. Called *Le Ballet Comique de la Reine*, it must have been a feat of production calling for great stamina and endurance.

Ballets such as these were performed in the grand hall of the palace with the audience sitting or standing on two sides. The king and his entourage would be seated at one end facing the dancers. The performers were recruited from the nobility with their peers sitting or standing in the audience. Dance was an essential part of court life and was taken very seriously, a great deal of time being spent perfecting the steps and movement.

Spectacle, patterns, elaborate costumes and settings were now added to the development of ballet. A focal point was established in 'facing the presence'. Ballet encompassed any form of entertainment which had patterns and development in movement. There were many famous ballets in which horses were used and both the animals and their riders were beautifully dressed. These magnificent spectacles, which originated from Italy, were staged in the open air and were the forerunners of the present day tournaments and tattoos. The beautiful exhibitions given by the horses of the Spanish Riding School in Vienna are also derived from the horse ballets of the seventeenth century.

It was during the reign of Louis XIV of France (1638–1715) that the court ballets reached their zenith. Louis was an enthusiastic dancer and first appeared in a ballet at the age of twelve. Part of his day was always allocated to a lesson with his dancing master and these lessons would often take precedence over matters relating to politics or affairs of state. Presented as part of magnificent court spectacles, ballets were evolved round the king and were made to emphasise his supreme power as ruler. One such ballet was *Le Ballet Royal de la Nuit* (1653) in which Louis portrayed Apollo, the Sun God, thus earning himself the title of the Sun King.

The Baroque period of the seventeenth and eighteenth centuries was a time of great elegance, during which it was considered fashionable to walk with slightly turned out feet. This influenced dance, and the straight parallel steps of the Italians gave way to what was known as the French style. The dancers also wore heeled shoes giving the body an added poise which, combined with the turn-out, gave an elegant line to the limbs and enabled them to execute the required steps with grace and ease. The vocabulary of steps was very small and consisted of only three steps, four springing movements, a falling step, a beat and a flourish. The names given to the various steps were: *jeté, assemblé, sis-*

11

sone and *pas tombé* and are still used in classical ballet technique today, although the execution is very different.

The social status of the professional entertainer before the seventeenth century was very low. During the Middle Ages, players were classed as acrobats, jugglers or buffoons and were on a level with outcasts and vagrants. They were often hounded by the law and even excommunicated by the Church. The professional entertainers employed in the ballets and spectacles of the seventeenth century were only used to portray grotesque characters or monsters and were certainly not allowed to dance using the court technique, which was reserved for the nobility alone. In England, these performers would appear before the start of a masque to highlight the beauty of the spectacle to follow. It is interesting to speculate on how the professionals and well-bred amateurs mixed in the strict social structure of that time.

Louis's great dancing masters were Pierre Beauchamp (1636–1719) and Louis Pécour (1653–1729) who both helped to establish the court techniques of their day. In 1661 Louis founded L'Académie Royale de Danse and appointed thirteen dancing masters to work there. These masters wished to formalise each dance into a set pattern which only they were authorised to teach and they succeeded in this with the minuet. However, disagreements prevented other court dances from becoming similarly circumscribed.

Eight years later, Louis instituted L'Académie de Musique, which was the foundation of the Paris Opéra. A school of dance was eventually established there in 1713 and it was from here, rather than L'Académie Royale de Danse, that ballet in France developed.

One of the king's favourites was the Italian composer Jan Baptiste Lully (1632–87), who eventually became Director of L'Académie Royale de Musique. Originally a dancer, he composed music and wrote many scores for the court ballets.

Louis's retirement as a performer in 1670, initiated a great change in court entertainments. His courtiers appeared less and less and the noble art of dancing, as it was known, began to develop as a professional art. For the first time the professional dancers appeared not just as monsters but in various roles, including the once 'noble roles' played by the king. The technique used in the court ballets was the same as in social dances but the professionals, through their training, possessed a greater measure of flexibility. They also had a greater sense of showmanship and began to add technical tricks. With the arrival of professional ballet, the performances transferred from the court to the theatre and so ballet, for the first time, became a theatre performance with professional dancers. The performances always included a mixture of opera and dance, creating a form of entertainment which was to last for over half a century.

Another important development in the history of dance was the first appearance on stage of the female dancer. Previously the female roles had been danced by men but in 1681, Mlle de Lafontaine (1655–1738), together with three other dancers, Mlles Fanon, Roland and Lepeintre, danced in Lully's *Le Triomphe de l'Amour*. The history of the ballerina had begun. Mlle de Lafontaine was destined to dance with great success for ten years, after which she retired from the Paris Opéra and became a nun. She was succeeded by Marie Subligny (1666–1736) who had the distinction of being the first ballerina to dance in England, where she appeared in the years from 1700 to 1702. She was the first of many to visit London, although they were often criticised as being past their peak, too old or too fat.

Although ballerinas were admired for their grace and beauty and the quality of their movements, they were restricted by the floor length of their skirts as well as the cut and design of their costumes. The male dancers had more freedom allowed by their dress and were able to embellish their steps with beats and *entrechats* (a quick passing of the feet whilst still in the air) and this gave them a great advantage over ballerinas. However, not to be outclassed by the men, Marie Camargo (1710–70) mastered the very tricky beaten step and, in order to execute it successfully, she shortened her skirt to above the ankle, which was considered very daring. After the initial shock to audiences, this became the accepted length for a ballerina's skirt.

Camargo's light, quick and vivacious style of dancing established the virtuosity of the ballerina. It was she that first took the precaution of wearing drawers, known as *caleçon de precaution*, under her shortened skirt as a safety measure. A few years previously an unfortunate dancer, Mlle Mariette, caught her dress on a piece of scenery and revealed all to her astonished audience. It was from this incident and the wearing of precautionary drawers that a French slang term produced the word *tutu* (the shortened classical costume worn by ballerinas today).

Camargo was greatly admired and had a large and adoring public. In common with many dancers, past and present, she had a love of animals. In her retirement she surrounded herself with numerous cats, dogs and birds.

Marie Camargo, the eighteenth-century ballerina, as painted by Lancret. She was the first dancer to shorten her skirts in order to display the virtuosity of her footwork.

The other great ballerina of that time and a rival of Camargo was Marie Sallé (1707-56). She also was a frequent visitor to London, where her dramatic gifts were as greatly admired as the brilliant technique of Camargo. Her contribution to the reform of the dress of the ballerina was to dispense with part of the hoopskirt, and she actually appeared at Covent Garden in 1734 in a thin muslin costume. The heavy wigs of the time were also discarded by her.

Although the ballerinas enjoyed immense popularity, it was still the male dancer who dominated the scene. He was still able to outshine the ballerina with virtuosity allowed by his dress. The great dancer Gaetano Vestris (1729-1808) and his son Auguste (1760-1842) became the most celebrated dancers of the eighteenth century.

Changes were continually being made, and dancers and choreographers were always searching, experimenting and devising new methods by which to further their art. By the middle of the eighteenth century, ballet had become separated from opera and at last became an independent form of entertainment. One of the innovators of the time was Jean-Georges Noverre (1727-1810) who reformed ballet by abandoning the masks and wigs worn by dancers and developing a freer costume, discarding the hoops and panniers. Under his direction, movement expressed characters and told stories and was not just a display of technique. He produced one hundred and fifty ballets in his lifetime, many of which involved stories. A new pattern and a form of ballet emerged which became known as the *ballet d'action*. This is the type of story ballet that we see today, although in his day they were danced with a different style and technique. Noverre also advocated the use of safety curtains (a law now strictly enforced in every theatre) as well as fire drills. In his day the risks of fire were very high. He was the author of a book, *Letters on Dancing and Ballets* (1760), which is still regarded as a dancer's classic and many of his theories are still used today.

Although Noverre has always been given the credit for the introduction of the *ballet d'action*, in England, Shrewsbury-born John Weaver (1673-1760) was also incorporating similar ideas into his ballets. His ambition was to create entertainments which he summarised neatly by writing 'the tale is carried forward by movements rather than words'. In Vienna, Franz Hilverding (1710-68) was doing likewise. Noverre's influence was considerable and it was one of his pupils, Jean Dauberval (1742-1806), who created in 1789, at the Grand Theatre, Bordeaux, the ballet *La Fille Mal Gardée*. This ballet broke away from the usual classical themes, then the basis of most ballets, and introduced an amusing story based on country life with rural characters. This was the theme followed by Marie Antoinette and her ladies when they played at being dairy maids in the *L'Hameau* which was built in the grounds of the palace of Versailles.

Dauberval in turn was to influence his pupil, Salvatore Viganò (1769–1821), who worked at La Scala and in Vienna and for whom Beethoven was to write his only ballet score, *Prometheus*.

The cultural world was changing and this was reflected in the ballets of the day. There was a general unrest in Europe, and in France the Revolution of 1789 brought to an end a society and an era with all its traditions. Following wars and upheavals of this kind there comes a period of rehabilitation. The scene is set for new ideas and developments. The age of minuets, sarabandes and *gigues* had ended and ballet began to change with the new regime. The transitional period brought different techniques and costumes. Previously dancers had always worn a heeled shoe but now soft, tight fitting slippers were worn, not unlike those worn by their professional acrobatic predecessors in the court ballets of the previous century. The costume, particularly for women, followed the neo-classic empire style, which allowed much more freedom of movement. As often happens, those who campaign for reforms are often shocked at the results. Noverre was horrified at the flimsy dresses worn by the dancers at the Paris Opéra.

With the pliable shoe, the forerunner of the modern ballet shoe, and the freedom given by the new costumes, a new form of technique began to emerge. In each century a great mind appears and in the nineteenth century for ballet it was Carlo Blasis (1797–1878). He was an Italian dancer and choreographer and in 1820 he set down a comprehensive system of technique. His school in Milan produced some very fine dancers and his teaching was to change the whole concept of ballet. It is from his written summaries of dancing that we have the classical techniques of today.

2
The Romantic Ballet

The nineteenth century was a period of great change. Europe was becoming more industrialised and a new class of society emerged which swept away many of the old traditions. In the ballrooms the waltz had appeared, which was thought scandalous by many, and in the theatre a new era had commenced. Artists rebelled against the rigid rules of classicism and the academic training of the previous century, and they also reacted violently against the growing materialism around them, resulting in a more emotional approach to their work.

The Romantic artists created worlds of fantasy and illusion as a reaction and the scene was set to change the world of ballet. Into this atmosphere came the first of the great ballerinas of the Romantic movement. In 1827, at the age of twenty-three, Marie Taglioni (1804–84) made her début at the Paris Opéra and so began a new epoch in dance. Taglioni was born in Stockholm, her mother was Swedish and her father an Italian dancer and choreographer. At that time the dancing and theatrical professions were confined to families who passed down their art from generation to generation, and it was from her father, Filippo Taglioni (1777–1871), that Marie received her vigorous and intensive training. For her début in Vienna she worked six hours daily over a period of six months. She was completely unlike the dancers of her time physically, being thin and delicate with a great grace and charm. She had a wonderful gift of elevation and it was in the ballet *La Sylphide*, which was created for her by her father, that the Romantic ballet reached its zenith. The critic of the French newspaper *Le Figaro* wrote 'Her début will open a new epoch', which proved to be a very accurate forecast. Lady Blessington, who was in the audience at Taglioni's first performance, said 'Her's is a totally new style of dancing, graceful beyond all comparison with a wonderful lightness and an absence of all violent effort, or at least the appearance of it, with a modesty that is as new as it is delightful to witness in her art. She seems to float and bound like a sylph.' Marie Taglioni's fame spread through Europe and she was soon recognised as the Queen of Romantic ballet.

17

Her most famous role was that of *La Sylphide*, a story set in Scotland which caught the imagination of the public at a time when the novels of Sir Walter Scott were all the rage. She also revolutionised the ballet costume by introducing the tight bodice and the full tarlatan net skirt—the classical tutu style as is still worn today.

The themes of the Romantic ballets dwelt on sylphs, wilis, fairy creatures and unearthly beings who, with the aid of stage machinery, appeared to be airborne. The supernatural quality was heightened by ballerinas standing on the tips of their toes to give the appearance of flight. The shoes were unblocked, unlike those worn today, and the dancers' toes were protected with padding. There is no definite record of when *pointe* was first performed but Taglioni was the first to use it artistically rather than as a trick. Taglioni's success influenced the music, stories and stage settings of ballets. Instead of choreographers writing the plots, well-known playwrights were now used; the most famous was Théophile Gautier (1811–72) who wrote the story of *Giselle*. Stage designers gained recognition as important contributors to ballet and stage sets included Gothic ruins, exotic scenes with mists, moonlight, sunsets and magical effects. All these factors created a perfect setting for the Romantic dancers.

The great age of the ballerina had begun and the adoration that they received could be compared to that of any present day pop star. In 1834 the Director of the Paris Opéra, an astute gentleman called Dr Véron, invited the Austrian dancer Fanny Elssler (1810–84) to appear as a counter attraction to Taglioni. Elssler was dark, dramatic and very beautiful, a complete contrast to her rival. She had already enjoyed huge success in Berlin and London and her appearance at the Paris Opéra created a great sensation. Dr Véron, with an eye for business, encouraged the rivalry between the two ladies and their admirers. Taglioni presented the image of the ethereal sylph defying the laws of gravity, whilst Elssler offered the dramatic side, as vividly shown by her passionate interpretation of the Spanish dance, *Cachucha*. Both of these ballerinas were in great demand and undertook arduous overseas tours which did much to stimulate interest in ballet.

While the two stars of the Paris Opéra were abroad, replacements had to be found to satisfy the French audiences. This was no easy task, but at this time, a talented Italian dancer called Carlotta Grisi (1819–99) appeared. Grisi was to become one of the greatest dancers of her day and was acclaimed for her performance in *Giselle*. This ballet was written for her by Gautier, who wrote, 'She reminds me of a tea rose about to bloom. She has a well proportioned body which, although slender and light, has nothing of that attenuated anatomy which so often makes dancers resemble racehorses in training—all bone and muscle.' Grisi was discovered and promoted by a French dancer and choreographer called Jules Perrot (1810–92), who was one of the most prolific artists of his day. A student of Auguste Vestris, he had partnered Taglioni for a short time until he received more applause than her and was quickly replaced!

The first production of *Giselle* is credited to Jean Coralli (1779–1854), the contemporary resident choreographer at the Opéra, and the solos were arranged for Grisi by Perrot. *Giselle* was to become the most widely known of the Romantic ballets, and remains one of the most popular works of the present day.

London, like other European capitals, had a large ballet public who saw many exciting performances. In the early years of her reign, Queen Victoria had greatly admired the ballerinas who appeared at Her Majesty's Theatre and in 1843 she expressed a wish to see Fanny Elssler and an Italian ballerina, Fanny Cerrito (1817–1909) in a *pas de deux*. This royal command presented a problem: neither dancer wished to appear first thus giving precedence to the other. Perrot, who was then choreographer at Her Majesty's Theatre, arranged an opening sequence in which both the ballerinas danced the same steps together. A piece of diplomacy which must have been appreciated by the Queen.

This performance was a great success and prompted Mr Lumley, the manager, to present a performance which required four ballerinas. Another diplomatic triumph secured the services of Taglioni, Cerrito, Grisi and a young Danish ballerina, Lucile Grahn (1819–1907). Perrot arranged a *Pas de Quatre*, in which Taglioni as senior ballerina had the final solo and Grahn, as the most junior, appeared first. Then came the problem of second and third placings but finally Grisi had second place. Perrot, if not gifted as a choreographer, would obviously have made his mark in the diplomatic world. Only six performances were given but they were an outstanding success and flower petals descended upon the four ladies after each performance.

It was also in 1843 that Grisi presented her latest ballet, *La Péri*, to London audiences. One of the highlights of the ballet was when Grisi took a flying leap into her partner's arms. On this occasion the partner was Lucien Petipa (1815–98), brother of the choreographer Marius. However, one evening she misjudged the leap and stopped the music and informed the conductor that she would try again. The audience

19

begged her not to attempt a second try and a Cockney wit called from the gallery 'Give Petipa a glass of grog, he is shaking on his pins'. The second attempt was successful.

From 1847 the ballet in Europe began to decline. The new ballerinas did not have the same quality, the public were always looking for something different and the success of *Pas de Quatre* was hard to surpass. With the advent of Jenny Lind, the Swedish nightingale, the public flocked to the opera and although the ballet was to survive for several more years it was gradually reduced to a divertissement in the opera and a main feature only in music halls.

During the Romantic period the role of the ballerina was enhanced, but the role of the male dancer diminished and male roles were often danced by women. When *Coppélia* was first performed in Paris in 1870, the part of Franz was danced by one of the prettiest girls in the company and until quite recently this role was danced *en travesti* at the Paris Opéra. The one flaw in the Romantic ballet period was that it obscured the role of the male dancer. Although Perrot and many others did appear in productions, they were mainly only required to support the ballerinas or play character or demi-character parts; the attention was always focussed on the ballerina. A prejudice against the male dancer had arisen from the audiences of that time. His role in nineteenth-century ballet was not understood or appreciated, unlike the period of Louis XIV, when the male dancer was supreme. Gautier described a male dancer as 'a man who shows his red neck, his powerful muscular arms, his legs with the calves of a parish beadle—all his strong and massive frame shaken by leaps and pirouettes.' No doubt an exaggeration, but even so, not exactly a Romantic figure. This prejudice lasted well into the twentieth century and even today there is a measure of opposition to a boy who wishes to learn ballet dancing. During the *travesti* period, ballet often became a caricature of its previous glory and it was many years before the balance was restored between male and female dancers.

3
The Russian Ballet and its Influence

Music, song and dance have always been an integral part of the background and life of the Russian people. The Russians had a great love of entertainments and the theatre but before the eighteenth century they relied on foreign companies or amateurs to provide the performances. There was no permanent school or company, as in Paris, and many of the rich landowners used the peasants to entertain guests with folk songs and dances. It was not until 1738 that the first Imperial Ballet School was created by the Empress Anna Ivanovna. The pupils were chosen from the children of the servants and from this time was founded the long tradition of dance which exists today.

The first ballet master and director of the Imperial School was a Frenchman, Jean Baptiste Landé (?-1748), and it was he that laid the foundations of Russian Ballet. Over the years he established the first links with foreign dancers and teachers. Landé's instructions were to teach on Mondays, Tuesdays, Thursday and Friday afternoons and to teach with 'honesty, sincerity, seriousness and with all the qualities of a good man'. He remained in Russia for many years and through his tireless efforts the first Russian company emerged.

It was another Empress, Catherine the Great, who had a great love of the arts, that re-established the Imperial School, bringing together dance, music, drama and painting under one roof. During her reign the great Viennese ballet master, Hilverding, spent over five years in St. Petersburg, the Imperial capital, where he produced many court ballets with Russian themes as opposed to the endless Greek stories. When he retired through illness, his pupil, Gasparo Angiolini (1731–1803) became master. He was a talented teacher and choreographer and composed many of his own scores. Under the Imperial patronage ballet continued to flourish and maintained a link with Western civilisation.

Paris and all that was French was considered to be the height of fashion by the Russians. They copied French clothes, employed decorators and artists from France and were influenced by its architecture. As late as the twentieth century the French jeweller, Carl Fabergé (1846–

1920), was creating the most beautiful objects for the Russian court. French cooks and governesses were in great demand. It was therefore natural for the Russians to turn to France in matters relating to ballet, and their next visitor in 1801 was Louis Didelot (1767–1837). Apart from creating over fifty ballets, his value was in his contribution to the art of teaching. He had been trained in Paris by Auguste Vestris and therefore brought the best of teaching to the Russians.

Didelot was a hard worker and a harsh ballet master. During his twenty-five years in St. Petersburg he introduced many reforms and raised the standard of the ballet performances. A pupil said of him 'the greater his interest in one particular pupil the more attention was lavished on her. Often you could pick out a coming star by the bruises which she had as the slightest mistake was rewarded with a blow, slap or thump.' He was also not averse to standing in the wings during a performance and giving an offending dancer a good shake. Life under Didelot must have been a trial but he certainly obtained results.

The second major city in Russia was Moscow where ballet was also developing. It was here that it was first taught to children in the orphanage and although foreign artists were still in great demand, a generation of Russian dancers was developing. One of the outstanding Russian teachers and choreographers was Ivan Valberg (1766–1819), who worked in St. Petersburg and Moscow and who replaced Didelot on his retirement.

The enormous popularity of the Romantic ballet in Europe also reached Russia. Marie Taglioni was the first of the great ballerinas to appear and her performance in *La Sylphide*, in St. Petersburg on the 6th September 1837, was a sensation. So popular were her appearances that she made return visits over the next five years and was a great inspiration to Russian dancers. She also helped to revive a waning interest in ballet, which had been going through a slight decline.

The adoration that Taglioni aroused was extraordinary and taken to great lengths. A group of her admirers obtained a pair of her shoes, cooked them, served them with a sauce and ate them. She returned to Europe laden with jewels and sables and no doubt the Customs of the time were very lenient with her!

Taglioni's appearances were followed by those of Grahn and Elssler. They were also greatly admired, and at Elssler's final performance in Moscow students drew her carriage through the streets.

With the decline of ballet in Europe during the mid-nineteenth century, Russia benefited. Perrot, well-known to London audiences, presented many of his famous ballets in St. Petersburg. He was followed by Arthur Saint-Léon (1821–70), the French dancer and choreographer remembered for his ballet *Coppélia* which was first produced at the Paris Opéra.

During the uncertainty of the times in Europe, Russia must have seemed heaven to artists. The next great influence to appear was the Frenchman Marius Petipa (1818–1910), who came from a generation of dancers. His brother Lucien was the first dancer to appear as Albrecht in *Giselle*. Petipa first appeared in Russia as a dancer but in 1869 he was appointed as chief ballet master to the Imperial company in St. Petersburg. He held the appointment for thirty-four years and during this period created over sixty full-length ballets. This term of office would not have been easy if the Tsar had not been inclined towards the arts, as the school and all the dancers were dependent upon the patronage of the Crown.

During Petipa's reign as choreographer, a set pattern for the ballet became established. A work was expected to have three or four acts, numerous scene changes and transformations and processions were essential for the display of elaborate costumes. In the centre of all this magnificence there was the ballerina. The *corps de ballet* would appear and perform various national dances and set the stage to highlight the ballerina who expected to have a solo or a *pas de deux* in each act. Petipa planned his ballets meticulously and moved his dancers through complicated patterns and plots. Ballets such as *The Sleeping Beauty*, *Raymonda*, *La Bayadère*, *Don Quixote* are all still performed today although in more up-to-date versions.

The training of the Russian dancers was steadily improving and both in St. Petersburg and Moscow the technical as well as the artistic standards were developing. There had been periods when standards had fallen below par and Nicholas I, after a visit to the Imperial School, said 'Even my dogs lead a better life than these dear little things'. Both cities possessed some fine dancers although foreign guest stars were still imported for major roles. It was essential at this time to present a star ballerina if a performance was to be a success. The public tended to lose interest unless they saw exceptional talent. There was also the additional value of the inspiration given to the Russian dancers by visiting artists.

Italy, and especially Milan, had become the centre of teaching, and when the Italian dancer Virginia Zucchi (1849–1930) arrived in St. Petersburg in 1885 she thrilled her Russian audiences with her Latin

23

temperament, dramatic ability and strong technique. Other Italian dancers were to follow and a few years later Carlotta Brianza (1867–1930), a pupil of Blasis, was to create the role of Aurora in Petipa's masterpiece *The Sleeping Beauty* whilst the male role of the Bluebird in this ballet was danced by Enrico Cecchetti (1850–1928).

The Imperial Ballet was so impressed by the strong techniques of these two artists that Cecchetti was invited to teach at the Imperial School and so began a great career of teaching as well as dancing.

The Sleeping Beauty was also a musical landmark heralding the introduction of the work of symphonic composers into the ballet world. Tchaikovsky's (1840–93) lovely score for this ballet is one of his most famous and popular works. Following the example set by Tchaikovsky, Glazunov (1865–1936) composed a fine score for *Raymonda* in 1898. Tchaikovsky also wrote scores for *The Nutcracker* (1892) and *Swan Lake* (1875). Unfortunately both of these ballets suffered from indifferent productions and they would have disappeared completely but for the music.

Swan Lake was first produced in Moscow but the choreography by the resident ballet master was not very distinguished, the dancing was not of a very high standard and the conductor was unable to appreciate the symphonic score: the ballet music of the time was not outstanding. The ballet was very quickly dropped and it was not until 1895, after many trials and tribulations that the complete four acts were presented at the Maryinsky theatre in St. Petersburg. Sadly, Tchaikovsky did not live to see his masterpiece performed as he had died tragically from cholera a year earlier. The choreography was partly by Petipa and partly by Lev Ivanov (1834–1901), the assistant ballet master. Ivanov had always been overshadowed by the great Petipa and he was to die penniless and forgotten.

The ballerina role of Odette/Odile was danced by an Italian virtuoso Pierina Legnani (1863–1923) who was able to perform thirty-two *fouettés*, a technical feat impossible to the Russian ballerinas of the time and a trick which has plagued the ballet ever since.

In 1903 Petipa, who was eighty-five, retired after a lifetime of service at the Maryinsky. The Imperial Ballet now had a system of training which was based on both the French and Italian methods and which had been adapted to suit the Russian temperament. New dancers who could equal the foreign stars were at last emerging. One of these was Mathilde Kschessinska (1872–1971), who rose to the exalted position of *prima ballerina assoluta*, a title achieved by only very few dancers. She was the first Russian ballerina to dance the role of Aurora in *The Sleeping Beauty* and to execute the thirty-two *fouettés* in *Swan Lake*.

At the beginning of the twentieth century there were many new ideas and aesthetic principles involving all the arts, especially in music and painting. These were outlined in an influential art magazine called *The World of Art* (*Mir Isskustva*) which was edited by a young law student, Serge Diaghilev (1872–1929) in collaboration with two brilliant painters, Alexandre Benois (1870–1960) and Léon Bakst (1866–1924).

With the contemporary changes in the arts it was natural that there should be a reaction in the ballet world, but Petipa's pattern had been firmly established and the Imperial theatres saw no reason to change. This attitude was strongly criticised by *The World of Art*. The ballet had brilliant dancers such as Kschessinska, Olga Preobrajenska (1870–1962), Anna Pavlova, Julie Sedova (1880–1970), Tamara Karsavina (1885–1979) and Nicolas Legat (1869–1937) but the ballets were considered old fashioned. Benois wrote, 'we certainly have no intention of running down Petipa's talents for he has been responsible for some lovely groupings, but there is a large gap between this and true art. There is nothing here but pretty little pictures with no depth and without expression.' At about this time, a young dancer and choreographer, Mikhail Fokine (1880–1942), who had been trained in the Imperial School, gained prominence. He believed that ballet should aim for a greater naturalness, just as Noverre had advocated in the eighteenth century, and felt that every ballet should have a style of movement suitable to its theme, country and period. He wanted to reform the long mime interludes and let movement convey the dramatic content and he wished to use the *corps de ballet* as part of the action instead of in its decorative role. His proposed reforms also included both costumes and music. These revolutionary ideas did not receive the approval of the Imperial School but after a great struggle his first ballet, *Le Pavillon d'Armide*, was eventually performed at the Maryinsky Theatre. It proved to be a great success and revealed a creator with great gifts. Fokine had used the young Benois to create the décor and it was through him that Fokine was introduced to Diaghilev. The ideas published in *The World of Art* and of its editor were much in line with those of the choreographer.

During the period 1906–08 Diaghilev had presented a series of exhibitions, concerts and opera performances in Paris, all exploiting Russian art. These had aroused such interest that he was encouraged to present some of Russia's greatest opera and ballet stars. He invited

Tamara Karsavina was one of the world's most loved ballerinas and was creator of many roles with the Diaghilev Ballet Russe. Her beauty and artistry were outstanding.

26

artists from St. Petersburg and Moscow during their summer vacation to come to Paris. These included Pavlova, Karsavina, Bronislava Nijinska, Adolph Bolm (1884–1951), Vaslav Nijinsky (1888–1950), Mikhail Mordkin, Laurent Novikov (1888–1956) and Fokine.

At the first performance on the 18th May 1909, there was a programme consisting of *Le Pavillon d'Armide* and the dances from *Prince Igor*. From this date onwards ballet in the West was changed. Paris had never seen such fine dancing, such colour or such a blending of all the arts. The show of skill and virtuosity by the male Russian dancers was almost wholly responsible for the restoration of the importance of the male dancer in Western ballet.

The success of this short season was followed by another and then in 1911 Diaghilev decided to break with Russia and tour Europe with a permanent company. Some of his dancers decided to leave the Imperial theatres to join him although others returned home. Karsavina became the chief ballerina for the new company and Nijinsky, the finest male dancer of his time, became premier danseur. Fokine worked as chief choreographer and Benois and Bakst were responsible for producing the most colourful costumes and scenery. The repertoire began with *Les Sylphides*, a ballet in the romantic style which had been choreographed by Fokine for the students at St. Petersburg and was then called *Chopinianna*. This was followed by *The Firebird*, a sensational ballet based on a Russian fairy story with music by Igor Stravinsky (1882–1971), the oriental *Schéhérazade, Petrushka, Daphnis and Chloë* and other ballets. Wherever the company appeared they were an immediate success and Bakst's sense of colour was to influence artists, interior decorators, painters and even women's fashions. Diaghilev's Ballet Russe, as the company was named, was to exist for twenty years and in this time the greatest of creative artists were to work for him. Diaghilev possessed a gift for bringing together the finest dancers, musicians and artists and he was able to discover, develop and extend young talent. Never content to rest on past success, he constantly sought new ideas and methods for the ballet, all of which equated with the outlook of musicians and painters of the early twentieth century.

Naturally many of his experiments were not successful and some new ballets only lasted for a season, but others became masterpieces. A Diaghilev season was never dull and each production was the result of a brilliant combination of talent. Such an assembly of artistic temperament led to some dissension and there was much coming and going among Diaghilev's team, which resulted in a constant search for new

Vaslav Nijinsky, the first of the great Russian male dancers to have a sensational success in the West.

talent. His great strength lay in not being dependent upon one artist, realising that an over-ruling genius can often hamper the growth of a company.

When Fokine left, Diaghilev encouraged Nijinsky to try choreography and his first ballet, *L'Après-midi d'un Faune* with music by Claude Debussy (1862–1918), was produced in 1912. In his choreography, Nijinsky broke away from the classical dance style and invented a new method of movement. In *L'Après-midi d'un Faune* the dancers moved in a two dimensional profile, flat footed and turned in, and they did not follow the musical phrasing. Ernst Ansermet (1883–1969), who conducted for the ballet, wrote that 'Diaghilev was quite unsatisfied with the choreography. Debussy's idea of the faun was very flexible and Nijinsky had made mechanical choreography. It was a dream of a summer afternoon: with Nijinsky the erotic side came too much into the light.' The next year Nijinsky choreographed *Jeux* and Stravinsky's *Sacre du Printemps*. The latter caused a riot at its first performance due to the unfamiliar sounds and rhythms of the music coupled with the strange inverted movements of the dancers. Nijinsky's choreography coincided with the Cubist movement in painting with which it had much in common and his ballets began to show the beginnings of a contemporary dance style which was to flourish many years later.

After only ten years with the company Nijinsky left the Ballet Russe in 1913 when he was only twenty-nine years old. In the next four years he danced briefly but he was to suffer, tragically, from a mental illness until the end of his life.

Through the difficult years of World War I Diaghilev recruited new talent and for the first time employed dancers that were not Russian. Lydia Sokolova (1896–1974) was the first English dancer to join the company, changing her name from Hilda Munnings. Leon Woizikovsky (1897–1975) and Stanislas Idzikowski (1894–1977) were both very fine male dancers from Poland. From Russia there was Vera Nemchinova (1899–) and from the Bolshoi Ballet in Moscow, Leonide Massine (1895–1979). Massine succeeded Nijinsky and proved not only to be an excellent dancer but also a talented choreographer. Two of his most famous works, *The Three Cornered Hat* and *La Boutique Fantasque*, created much excitement for post-war audiences.

Paris was still the centre of the art world, enabling Diaghilev to use the finest of composers and artists. For his ballet scores he commissioned music from Francis Poulenc, Georges Auric, Darius Milhaud, Serge Prokofiev, Constant Lambert and Lord Berners. For designers he chose

29

Leonide Massine, one of Diaghilev's most outstanding dancers and a brilliant choreographer. He is shown here as the Hussar in his famous ballet, Le Beau Danube.

Picasso, Matisse, Gris, Braque, Derain, Miro, Tchelitchev and Chirico. His company reflected the arts of his period.

In 1921–22 Diaghilev presented an elaborate re-staging of the great Russian classic *The Sleeping Beauty* (called by him *The Sleeping Princess*). This nearly brought about the financial collapse of the company (an ever present danger). The public were used to short, entertaining ballets and a large scale production on Imperial lines was beyond them. It was many years before this ballet became accepted although it is now one of the most popular works of the present day.

Diaghilev's insight was to find him yet another gifted choreographer, Nijinsky's sister Bronislava Nijinska (1891–1972). She had worked with the company before the war but re-joined it for the production of *The Sleeping Princess*. In ballets such as *Les Biches* and *Le Train Bleu* she evoked the atmosphere of the 1920s and in *Les Noces*, to Stravinsky music, she created the atmosphere of a Russian wedding.

Inevitably Nijinska left the company and was replaced, in 1924, by a young Russian dancer, George Balanchine (1904–). For Diaghilev, Balanchine was to create several works, including *Apollo* and *The Prodigal Son*. Both of the male roles in these ballets were created by a young Russian dancer, Serge Lifar (1905–), who had joined the company in 1923. By this time the company had become truly international and included several English dancers, all with international names: Anton Dolin (1904–), renamed from Patrick Healey-Kay, joined in 1924; Ninette de Valois (1898–), born Edris Stannus, joined in 1923 and Alice Marks, now Alicia Markova (1910–), joined in 1925. Unfortunately the days of the Ballet Russe were numbered and with Diaghilev's death in 1929 an incredible era ended.

During this era the undoubted great influences in the world of ballet were Diaghilev and Anna Pavlova (1881–1931). She had joined the Ballet Russe in its early days but left it to form her own company and tour the world. It was a much smaller company than Diaghilev's Ballet Russe but this gave it the advantage of mobility and enabled it to reach countries which had never heard of ballet. Pavlova adapted her ballets to her audiences and inspired many to become dancers. Her death, a few years after Diaghilev's, concluded an era in which ballet had regained its place among the arts.

Following his death, Diaghilev's artists set out to form companies and to teach, thus sustaining the interest that had been won both by him and Pavlova. In the early 1930s two impresarios, Colonel W. de Basil (1888– 1951) and René Blum (1878–1942) gathered together many of Diaghilev's

Anna Pavlova, one of the most outstanding personalities of ballet. She toured the world with triumphant success in countries that had never seen ballet before.

dancers and ballets in order to form a new Ballet Russe. In the Paris studios three very charming young ballerinas were discovered who became known as the baby ballerinas. They were Tatiana Riabouchinska (1917-), Tamara Toumanova (1919-) and Irina Baronova (1919-). All three had been trained by former ballerinas of the St. Petersburg Imperial Ballet who had been compelled to flee to France at the time of the Russian Revolution.

The new company shone with personalities and was headed by the sparkling Danilova and the gifted Massine. A new departure was set by Massine when he used symphonic music for ballets and such favourites as *Le Beau Danube* and *Gaieté Parisienne* were featured. As was to be expected in this world of impressarios and dancers, things did not run smoothly and there were the inevitable departures from the company. René Blum and Massine left to form their own companies which toured extensively, proving to be as popular as their seasons were exciting. Each company kept a wary eye on the other, assessing the rival programmes being given, dancers in the company, etc. This rivalry was an incentive and sometimes the two companies would appear in the same city at the same time. On one occasion in London, the de Basil company was at the Royal Opera House and Massine was at the Theatre Royal, Drury Lane, only a few minutes away. Balletomanes would endeavour to fit in both performances by running from one theatre to the other during the intervals.

At the outbreak of World War II the companies were disbanded and eventually were re-formed in America. The long tours that followed continued to sustain, as well as to develop ballet.

Tragically René Blum became a victim of Nazi oppression and died in a concentration camp in Auschwitz.

Diaghilev, Pavlova, Nijinsky, Karsavina, Massine and Blum are all names that have conveyed to the world the beauty and art of the Russian Ballet.

4
The Ballet Worldwide

Great Britain

The English have always been excellent dancers and during Elizabethan times the nimbleness of foot earned them the title of 'The Dancing English'. Foreign visitors to London were taken to see the young men practising the *Galliard*, an energetic dance requiring intricate footwork and elevation. Many visitors were shocked however when they saw Queen Elizabeth and her ladies dancing *La Volta*, in which they were lifted up into the air by their partners showing rather too much ankle and petticoat.

In 1717 John Weaver created the first English *ballet d'action* when his ballet *The Loves of Mars and Venus* was staged at the Theatre Royal, Drury Lane in London.

In the nineteenth century the Romantic ballerinas achieved some of their greatest successes in London and, following the decline in popularity of ballet in Europe, prestigious productions at the Alhambra and Empire music halls maintained high standards and presented ballet to a totally new public. These performances were very lavish and considered to be the finest in Europe. They featured some of the outstanding dancers of the time and were excellent examples of Victorian art.

One of the ballerinas to appear at the Empire theatre was Adeline Genée (1878–1970) who arrived in London with a six-week contract and stayed for ten years, an indication of her popularity.

Although dancers were being trained in Britain, there was no national company, and employment had to be found in the music-hall ballets, musical comedies or Pavlova's company. Pavlova had a great love of London and her studio and home were on the outskirts of the capital. Her home is now a museum.

It was two very energetic and far-sighted dancers, Marie Rambert (1888–) and Ninette de Valois (1898–) who were to create the first British companies. Both had at different times worked in the Diaghilev company.

Born in Warsaw, Rambert had studied Dalcroze eurhythmics in

Geneva and Dresden. Because of this training, Diaghilev invited her to join his company to help Nijinsky with the difficult Stravinsky score for *Sacre du Printemps* or *Rite of Spring*. The eurhythmics were of great value, enabling her to explain the changing time signatures, the counts and uneven phrasing, Nijinsky, who often had premonitions about the future, told Rambert 'Do not stay with the Diaghilev company, this is not the place for you! Your work will lie elsewhere.' Taking this advice to heart, Rambert left the Diaghilev company and during World War I went to London where she married Ashley Dukes the author.

In 1920 she opened a school in London where one of her first pupils was Frederick Ashton (1904-   ). He had spent his childhood in South America, where his parents were living, and during one of Pavlova's tours he had been taken to see her dance in Peru. Inspired by this great ballerina he was determined to become a dancer and so came to London to study.

From her hard-working pupils Rambert formed a group of dancers, who, in 1930, became the Ballet Rambert, the first British ballet company. In the early days performances were given on Sundays at the Mercury Theatre, a converted church hall in Notting Hill Gate. The Ballet Club, as it was known, provided a setting for dancers and choreographers. They developed on the tiny stage a whole range of talent. Many of the dancers were working in musical shows as well as studying and rehearsing at the Mercury for the Sunday performances. Eventually Rambert was able to form a company which could offer permanent work.

Like Diaghilev, Rambert possessed a great gift for finding and developing talent in others and her school and company became the nursery of British ballet. Although they were always working on a financial shoestring her company undertook many pioneer tours, often under very difficult conditions. It was one of the first companies to visit munition factories and military camps during World War II.

As is usual in the ballet world there were always comings and goings with both dancers and choreographers. Although sad to see them go Rambert always realised that talented members of her company needed larger stages and companies in order to expand.

Among her discoveries were such names as Frederick Ashton, Antony Tudor, Walter Gore, Frank Staff and Andrée Howard. These choreographers gave the company a repertoire ranging from the dramatic to the amusing. Many of the ballets of that time have become landmarks in the history of ballet and are still performed today. Many choreographers have received their inspiration from such works as

35

Tudor's *Dark Elegies*, *Lilac Garden* and *Gala Performance*; Howard's *Mermaid*, *Lady Into Fox* and *La Fête Etrange* (the latter is now performed by the Royal Ballet and considered to be a masterpiece); Staff's witty *Peter and the Wolf* and *Czernyanna*; Gore's *Simple Symphony* and *Winter Night*; and Ashton's *Façade* and *Capriol Suite*.

The dancers were trained in the classical technique but Rambert managed to develop artistic and interpretative qualities which enabled them to present a wide range of roles. The strength of her company lay in the smaller story ballets rather than the classics which require a larger company, but her production of *Giselle* has never been surpassed.

So many noted dancers passed through her company, such as Maude Lloyd, Sally Gilmour, Pearl Argyle, Elisabeth Schooling, Paula Hinton, Joyce Graeme, Belinda Wright, Lucette Aldous, Harold Turner, Hugh Laing and John Gilpin.

In 1966 the company changed its policy and its image. Rambert realised that with the interest that was being shown in the contemporary dance style she would have to develop the company along different lines. Her co-director Norman Morrice (1931–) was already introducing a modern approach in his choreography and had also invited the American choreographers, Glen Tetley (1926–) and Anna Sokolow (1915–) to produce works. A strong modern repertoire was being built up. New choreographers came from the dancers such as Jonathan Taylor and Christopher Bruce. Today, the company is devoted entirely to contemporary works.

Irish-born Ninette de Valois (it was the practice then for English dancers to adopt foreign names) had been a soloist in the Diaghilev company for two years, but in 1925 she decided to leave and open a school in London. Like Rambert's school, the pupils were to form the nucleus of a company. However, de Valois visualised ballet on a much larger scale and considered the possibility of establishing a national company in a permanent setting. To achieve this, she first needed a home base for her company. At this time, the formidable Lilian Baylis (1874–1937), the legendary figure who was running the Old Vic theatre, was planning to re-open the old Sadlers Wells Theatre as an opera centre. She welcomed de Valois's idea of dancers becoming the basis of a professional company there.

In 1931 the first major steps were taken and the Vic-Wells company was born. There was no lack of ambition and the great classic ballets, *Giselle*, *Swan Lake*, *Coppélia* and *The Nutcracker* were presented. These productions were given great strength and support by the two leading

Ninette de Valois famed as the founder of the Royal Ballet. She was a distinguished soloist with the Diaghilev Ballet Russe and other companies.

dancers, Alicia Markova (1910–) and Anton Dolin (1904–). Both were former dancers with the Diaghilev company and their presence helped, especially with the classics, to establish the Vic-Wells.

When Markova and Dolin left in 1935 to form their own company, replacements had to be found; a recurring problem which has often produced amazing results. In 1934 a fourteen year old girl had arrived from Shanghai to audition for the school and a year later she was accepted into the company. De Valois had an eye for talent and pinned her hopes on the young Margot Fonteyn (1919–) who made her modest début as a snowflake in *The Nutcracker* and was later to become one of the world's greatest ballerinas.

The Australian dancer, Robert Helpmann (1909–) had also joined the company and formed a most successful partnership with Fonteyn which was to last for many years. Helpmann's experience and showmanship gave tremendous confidence to Fonteyn and enabled her to develop as an artist.

De Valois had Ashton as a resident choreographer and the invaluable help of Constant Lambert (1905–51) the composer and conductor. She also had a young company of dancers who were steadily gaining strength and artistry. She herself choreographed many ballets including *Job*, *The Rake's Progress* and *Checkmate*, all of which are still performed today.

Ashton's early ambition was to be a dancer such as the fabled Nijinsky, but a fortune teller predicted that he would find success in another direction. The early ballets that he created for Rambert showed his choreographic talent and this gradually developed until he became the greatest British choreographer. For Fonteyn he was to choreograph her greatest roles outside of the classical repertoire. Their partnership did not have an auspicious beginning and in her autobiography she tells of complaining to her mother '"Frederick Ashton is absolutely mad, his steps are impossible!" He in turn complained to de Valois that I was very obstinate, a judgement that she shared—but she believed that I was very talented nevertheless'.

In 1940 the name of the company was changed to The Sadlers Wells Ballet. It toured extensively, building up a large public and helping to establish ballet as an art.

During the war years the Royal Opera House at Covent Garden had been converted into a dance hall but in 1946 it was re-opened and de Valois was invited to transfer her company there. A new production of *The Sleeping Beauty* was mounted for the occasion, a natural choice for de Valois to make as she had always been impressed with this ballet since she saw the Diaghilev version at the Alhambra. De Valois was indefatigable in developing young artists and, in spite of the move to the Royal Opera House, she maintained a small company at Sadlers Wells which she used to encourage a new generation of dancers and choreographers.

Helpmann, with his wonderful flair also produced several successful ballets and after his departure from the company in 1950 Michael Somes (1917–   ) became Fonteyn's partner. His career had been interrupted by military service.

Ashton's talent was no longer confined to small stages and he faced the challenge of the Opera House's immense space by creating *Symphonic Variations*, a ballet which has remained a masterpiece of classicism. The first cast of six were Margot Fonteyn, Pamela May, Moira Shearer, Michael Somes, Brian Shaw and Henry Danton. They expressed in lovely movement the beautiful César Franck (1822–90) music. The ballet had no story and the simplicity of the set and costumes showed to full advantage the quality and talent that had been developed in this company.

In 1956 the ballet *Birthday Offering* was created by Ashton for the twenty-fifth anniversary of the Sadlers Wells company, an occasion that revealed that it now had seven resident ballerinas. They were Margot Fonteyn, Beryl Grey, Violetta Elvin, Nadia Nerina, Svetlana Beriosova, Rowena Jackson and Elaine Fifield. Their partners were Michael Somes, Philip Chatfield, Desmond Doyle, Alexander Grant, Bryan Ashbridge, Brian Shaw and David Blair.

In 1956 the company was granted a royal charter, thus making it the Royal Ballet; a crowning achievement for Ninette de Valois.

Ashton continued to create excellent ballets for the company, making full use of the rising generation of dancers. For example, his adaptation of *A Midsummer Night's Dream*, called *The Dream* (1964), provided a worthy vehicle for the talented partnership of Antoinette Sibley (1939–   ) and Anthony Dowell (1943–   ). Earlier, in his re-creation of the old ballet *La Fille Mal Gardée* (1960) he had the assistance for the mime scenes, of the great ballerina Tamara Karsavina who had danced the role in St. Petersburg fifty years previously. This co-operation resulted in a role for Nadia Nerina (1927–   ) which lifted her to international stardom.

The following year saw the production of Ashton's *Les Deux Pigeons* (1961), choreographed for Lynn Seymour (1939–   ) and Christopher

Gable (1940–   ). All of Ashton's ballets have stood the test of time and are still performed today alongside his later works such as *Enigma Variations* and *A Month in the Country*.

The smaller company at Sadlers Wells also began to produce new dancers and choreographers. The South African-born John Cranko (1927–73) had already choreographed for the ballet company in Cape Town and his talent was encouraged by de Valois. His most successful ballet, which is still enormously popular today, was *Pineapple Poll*. Set to the music of Arthur Sullivan it was a comedy ballet full of demi-caractère dancing, telling the story of the handsome Captain Belaye and the pretty young Poll and the ups and downs of their romance in Portsmouth.

The dancer Kenneth MacMillan (1929–   ) was also to emerge as a major choreographer and his first important ballet was *Danses Concertantes* with Maryon Lane (1931–   ) and David Poole (1925–   ). He went on to create major ballets of great dramatic depth in which Lynn Seymour became his principal interpreter. Born in Canada, Seymour was chosen from the Royal Ballet *corps de ballet* to dance in *The Burrow* (1958). Her particular gifts as an actress and her exceptional ability as a ballerina, plus her powerful personality made her a pivot figure for MacMillan's work and he went on to create important ballets such as *Romeo and Juliet*, *Anastasia*, *Manon* and *Mayerling*.

The arduous tours of the Royal Ballet had won the company international acclaim. The dancers were praised, as was the presentation of the classical ballets and modern works. The English style of dancing had won world recognition as had the ability of the choreographers. Both the companies continued to maintain the very best in British ballet and other outstanding artists appeared, such as Merle Park, Lesley Collier, Marguerite Porter, David Wall, Michael Coleman, Wayne Eagling and Stephen Jefferies.

During the years in which the Ballet Rambert and the Sadlers Wells companies were developing, the interest in dance was also growing. Teaching societies were formed to guard and establish correctly the tuition of ballet dancing. The Royal Academy of Dancing grew out of an association formed in 1920, the Imperial Society of Teachers of Dancing had been founded in 1904 and the British Ballet Organisation in 1930.

Schools began to train some very fine dancers and new ballet companies began to appear. One of the first was the celebrated Markova-Dolin Ballet (1935–38) and this company toured extensively both in

Anton Dolin in Le Train Bleu, *a Diaghilev ballet especially created for him by Nijinska, with costumes by Chanel. He was the first to gain recognition in England for the male dancer.*

England and Europe.

Apart from Phyllis Bedells (1893–   ), who was the first English ballerina to appear at the Empire, it was Markova and Dolin who presented the ideal British classical partnership. Markova was the epitome of the classical ballerina and she was shown to advantage by the strength and style of Dolin. They both did much to establish ballet and Dolin kept the male role in perspective.

With the coming of World War II and the end of the Markova-Dolin company the Sadlers Wells and Ballet Rambert companies were the only two continuing to perform. However, in 1940 Mona Inglesby (1918–   ) formed the International Ballet with a repertoire of classics, as well as new works.

It toured successfully until 1953 and did much to stimulate an interest in ballet outside of London during the dismal war years and after.

The Anglo-Polish Ballet was another company which was formed in 1940, and their repertoire of Polish national dances, as well as their productions of *Swan Lake* and *Les Sylphides* proved very popular on their tours. During these difficult years the companies suffered extensively from bombings, black-outs, damaged theatres and impossible journeys with no hotels. Somehow these hardships were overcome.

One of the most popular companies today is the London Festival Ballet, a company which grew from a concert group formed by Markova and Dolin in 1949. This company has a very enthusiastic public and tours with great success both at home and overseas. They have journeyed as far afield as the Met. in New York and China.

Until 1979 its artistic director was the former Royal Ballet ballerina, Beryl Grey (1927–   ). She was the first British ballerina to appear both in Russia and China. John Field, also a Royal Ballet principal followed her as artistic director.

The repertoire of this company is varied and it includes the ever popular classics as well as several of Diaghilev's ballets such as *Schéhérazade*, *Prince Igor* and *Le Spectre de la Rose*. They also dance the Bournonville ballet *La Sylphide* as well as modern works by Tetley and Ronald Hynd.

For many years Galina Samsova and her husband André Prokovsky headed the company as did John Gilpin, one of the finest of English male dancers.

A small company formed by Elizabeth West and Peter Darrell in 1957 proved to be one of the most venturesome in Britain. Eventually it established a base in Scotland and became the Scottish Ballet. This

Alicia Markova, one of the greatest ballerinas, and the first British dancer to appear as Giselle and as Odette/Odile in Swan Lake *with the early Vic-Wells Ballet. She achieved enormous popularity and became an international name.*

company presents both classical and modern works and is very popular both in Britain and overseas.

The first regional dance company to be established in Britain is the Northern Dance Theatre. It is based in Manchester and tours the country with its repertoire of classical and modern ballets.

USA

During the nineteenth century many famous personalities of the theatre including singers, actors and dancers made the hazardous journey across the Atlantic to undertake long and arduous tours of North America.

The first of the great ballerinas to do such pioneer tours was Fanny Elssler, who, in 1840, arrived in New York fresh from her triumphs in Paris. She was extremely nervous about the kind of reception she would receive in the States but her fears were unfounded. Her performances were so successful that she toured for two years and returned home only because of family illness. When she appeared in Washington the House of Representatives finished its business early in order that the members should be able to see the famous ballerina perform. It is doubtful if this tribute would be paid to a dancer today.

Pavlova also toured tirelessly, as did Genée, and both presented ballet in towns and cities which had never seen this form of dance before. By today's standards their programmes would not be considered great art, but through their artistry and personalities these ballerinas introduced ballet to a new public as well as preparing the way for those that were to follow them. The New World offered great opportunities to artists and with the ending of the Diaghilev, Pavlova and de Basil companies many dance personalities decided to settle in the United States in order to teach and choreograph. One dancer, Mikhail Mordkin (1880–1944), a handsome and virile Russian who had done much to establish the importance of the male dancer, decided in 1923 to leave Europe and settle in the USA, where he founded a school. From this school he formed the Mordkin Ballet in 1937 and a year later it became a professional company with Lucia Chase, an American-born ballerina as principal dancer. It was from this company that the American Ballet Theatre developed, which Lucia Chase directed from its inception. It is through her devoted and personal efforts that this company has been sustained over the years.

At the beginning, this company consisted of many foreign dancers and teachers but it soon developed into an all-American company with

Alicia Alonso (1917–), the Cuban-born dancer as its brilliant ballerina. The policy has been to present a variety of ballets embracing the classics, Diaghilev works and contemporary ballets, the latter often with American themes. The company has always invited a series of guest stars and through its coast-to-coast tours it has enabled American audiences to see some of the finest dancers of this century.

The very diverse repertoire has attracted such artists as Rudolph Nureyev (1938–), Natalia Makarova (1940–) and Mikhail Baryshnikov (1948–), the English-born Anthony Dowell as well as the American dancers Fernando Bujones (1955–), Cynthia Gregory (1946–), Gelsey Kirkland (1953–) and Martine van Hamel (1945–). These are only a few of the great names that have been associated with this company. One of its original members, Nora Kaye (1920–), now an associate director, became the leading dramatic American ballerina of her time. Since her retirement in 1961 she has assisted her husband, Herbert Ross, in the production of musicals and successful films such as *The Turning Point* and *Nijinsky*. In 1939 the British choreographer, Antony Tudor was invited to help in the founding of the company and he re-produced such ballets as *Lilac Garden* and *Dark Elegies* which were part of the Rambert repertoire. Later he choreographed some of his finest works for the American Ballet Theatre and in which Kaye excelled as an interpreter. Tudor was able to convey subtle human relationships and situations which made his work memorable and gave the company an unique quality.

Another choreographer who had a great influence on the company was the American Jerome Robbins (1918–). Whilst still in the company he produced his first ballet *Fancy Free* (1944) and this helped to establish him as one of America's leading choreographers. The story of this ballet was of three sailors on leave in New York and from this came the successful musical film *On The Town*. The American theme, the music of Leonard Bernstein (1918–) and the choreographic treatment were to have a great influence on the American theatre and ballet. He has since created numerous ballets and directed musicals such as *West Side Story* which became a landmark in the history of the musical theatre.

Agnes de Mille (1909–) was another American choreographer who was attracted to home themes and American music, and for the American Ballet Theatre she produced some brilliant ballets such as *Rodeo*, with its cowboy theme and the exciting music of Aaron Copland (1900–), and *Fall River Legend* with music by Morton Gould (1913–). The latter was based on the story of Lizzie Borden who, in 1892, 'took an axe and gave her mother forty whacks; when she saw what she had done she gave her father forty one!'

The list of ballets performed by this company through the years is enormous and it has always been adventurous in its ideas, dancers and the choice of choreographers. In 1976, one of America's leading contemporary choreographers, Twyla Tharp (1942-) created *Push Comes to Shove*, a brilliant work to the mixture of a Haydn symphony and a Bohemian Rag of Joseph Lamb. This was the first work choreographed for Baryshnikov after he came to the West and his responsiveness to Tharp's quick, strange jazz movements brought him an overwhelming triumph.

Dancers tend to need a constant change and those of the American Ballet Theatre are no exception. It survives its losses and every season produces new talent and ideas.

Very different in style is the New York City Ballet, one of the leading ballet companies of the world. Its early beginnings and development are parallel with those of the American Ballet Theatre in that it is a company that grew out of a school run by an ex-Diaghilev dancer and choreographer, George Balanchine. In 1933 Lincoln Kirstein, a very distinguished art critic and writer, was determined to establish a great American company. He admired Balanchine's work and invited him to the States.

Through determination, hard work and overcoming many problems, a company finally emerged, but all of this had taken thirteen years and it was not until 1948 that it became established at the New York City Center, which gave the company its name.

Under the enthusiasm and direction of Kirstein the company gained tremendous prestige, and Balanchine created masterpieces of movement and line as well as musicality. His Russian background, Diaghilev experience and technical training, united with the American temperament resulted in an individual style which formed the identity of the company. As with the English style of the Royal Ballet, the Russian style of the Bolshoi and Kirov companies, there emerged the Balanchine type of dancer. His talent is exceptional and his output is vast: his ballets number over one hundred. Companies throughout the world have more than one of his works in their repertoire. The majority of his ballets are without plots; he sets out to interpret the music and evokes a wonderful feeling of dance in the classical style.

The typical Balanchine dancers show off his choreography to perfection. The women are slim, elegant and have long legs. His most famous dancers have included Maria Tallchief (1925–   ), the American ballerina who was a great exponent of his work, Tanaquil LeClerq (1929–   ), Melissa Hayden (1922–   ), Gelsey Kirkland, Suzanne Farrell (1945–   ), Violette Verdy (1933–   ) and Patricia McBride (1942–   ). There are many others who have also proved to be brilliant interpreters of Balanchine's work. His male dancers have also presented a wonderful image of the American dancer; two outstanding artists being Jacques d'Amboise (1934–   ) and Edward Villella (1936–   ). More recently the very fine Danish dancer Peter Martins (1946–   ) and Baryshnikov have been with the company. Although the repertoire is predominantly Balanchine, Jerome Robbins has also contributed some excellent works such as *Age of Anxiety*, *In the Night*, *Other Dances* and *Four Seasons*.

New York also has a smaller classical company which was formed in the early 1950s and eventually became the Joffrey Ballet, named after its director Robert Joffrey (1930–   ). It is a company which is trained in the classics and specialises in a repertoire of early ballets such as *The Green Table* by Kurt Jooss (1901–79), Ashton's *A Wedding Bouquet* and *Les Patineurs*, as well as his later ballet *The Dream*. They also dance modern works such as Twyla Tharp's *Deuce Coupe* and ballets by their resident choreographer Gerald Arpino (1928–   ).

Another company which enjoys great success on both sides of the Atlantic is the Dance Theatre of Harlem. This was founded by Arthur Mitchell (1934–   ) a former soloist with the New York City Ballet. Mitchell, a negro dancer of great promise, decided at the height of his career to devote his time to teaching. He was determined to give others of his race an opportunity to study dance. He opened his first school in a garage in Harlem. The school grew rapidly and he soon presented a fine team of dancers whose vitality, rhythm and sense of dance won them a great acclaim. Their repertoire includes part ethnic and part classical works.

Throughout the States there are many companies which are based on a region alone. Some are professional, others semi-professional or amateur. They all do valuable work offering dancers opportunities to perform as well as fostering and maintaining the art of ballet, in areas where major companies are rarely seen.

The oldest of the American professional companies is the San Francisco Ballet which was formed in 1933 by the émigré Adolf Bolm, a Russian dancer. Today, under the artistic direction of Lew Christensen (1908–   ) and Michael Smuin (1938–   ) it achieves outstanding success both on the west and east coasts of the United States as well as in tours

47

overseas. It has a large and varied repertoire, and it is by the latter that a company stands or falls.

American dance companies, perhaps more than those of other countries, maintain a continual change of ballets both old and new. It is this changing pattern that attracts dancers to work in the States.

USSR

Following the Revolution in 1917 the whole future of the ballet in Russia became very precarious. The new Government did not favour an art which had been so closely associated with the Imperial regime, and it was only through the persuasive powers of the new Commissar for Public Education, Anatoly Lunasharsky who was an ardent balletomane, that it was allowed to continue.

The years that followed were difficult, but gradually ballet began to thrive again and the classical works which had originally been mounted for the Tsar and his Court were performed again, although this time before a very different audience. To the old repertoire new ballets were added which had more realistic content and themes. *The Red Poppy* was a new work based on a story about Russian sailors and set against the background of the Chinese uprising. *Taras Bulba* was taken from a novel by Gogol in which the central figure was a medieval national hero. *Flames of Paris* dealt with the French Revolution, and *Spartacus* was the story of the revolt of slaves in ancient Rome. The Russians have always been avid readers of novels and choreographers turned for inspiration to such literary classics as *Romeo and Juliet*, and three-act ballets, with stories, have remained the basis of the Russian repertoire. This is a legacy from the Petipa/Tsarist days, and several much loved fairy stories have been made into successful ballets, such as *The Fountain of Bakhchisarai*, *The Little Humpbacked Horse*, *The Tale of the Stone Flower* and *Cinderella*, all of which are popular favourites.

Moscow had now become the capital city and old St. Petersburg became Leningrad. On the huge stages of the Bolshoi and the Kirov Theatres a new generation of dancers appeared who were to enthrall audiences with their wonderful dancing, in the same way that the Diaghilev and Pavlova companies had on their world tours. The Bolshoi company is one of the largest in the world with over two hundred dancers. Their productions are presented on a large scale with an impressive use of the number of dancers required for the ballets with stories.

The Bolshoi Ballet first appeared in London and the West in 1956 and their productions had to be adapted to fit the comparatively small stage of the Royal Opera House. The dancers revealed their unique style of dancing which was their inheritance stemming from a long tradition. This style, which distinguishes the Russians from the dancers of other countries, is based on the great teaching of the French and Italian schools combined with Russian teachers as interpreters of the technique. It was Agrippina Vaganova (1879-1951), a former ballerina at the Maryinsky theatre in St. Petersburg who formulated the system of teaching which is now used. Following the Revolution she devoted her time to teaching and was so successful that she was invited to become the chief teacher at the Leningrad State School. Her system was adopted and used throughout the USSR as well as in other countries in Eastern Europe. Her method of training develops very expressive bodies, arm movements and backs, together with high leaps and a sense of musicality.

The two major Soviet ballet companies, the Bolshoi and the Kirov, have visited many parts of the world and the wonderful quality of the dancers and their technique has been greatly admired. The two companies vary in their approach to style: the Bolshoi dancers tend to be stronger, more athletic and more emotional in interpretation, whereas the Kirov dancers are more lyrical, with a lightness and mobility that is outstanding. Both companies have produced some of the finest dancers in the world. Galina Ulanova (1910-) will be remembered for her poetic interpretations in the Bolshoi's *Romeo and Juliet* and *Giselle*. She has now retired from dancing but coaches some of the younger ballerinas in some of her famous roles.

Other outstanding ballerinas from the Bolshoi who have been seen in the West or on film are Raisa Struchkova (1925-), Maya Plisetskaya (1925-), Nina Timofeyeva (1935-), Ekaterina Maximova (1939-) and Marina Kondratieva (1934-).

The male dancer in Russia has always held an equal position to that of the ballerina. When ballet declined in popularity in western Europe the training of the male dancer was partially lost. In Russia this did not happen and in the first Diaghilev season in Paris the male dancers astounded the audiences. The Russian male develops a power to jump and cover space and his movements are expansive, all of which is necessary for the larger stages in the USSR. Dancers such as the legendary Nijinsky and Baryshnikov appear to defy gravity and seem to be able to suspend themselves in the air. The Russian ancestry embracing the Slav, Tartar and Cossack inheritance gives them a background of dance and an added magnetic personality and quality which eludes the dancers of the West.

The repertoires are classically based, and although new ballets are modern in choice of composer as well as choreographer, by western standards they are not considered contemporary. In the USSR, story ballets are preferred to the interpretive works, and these do not offer the variety or challenges of the latter. As a result, several dancers have wished to extend their range beyond the Soviet repertoires, and three of the Kirov's famous stars, Rudolph Nureyev, Natalia Makarova and Mikhail Baryshnikov, have left their native country to work in the West. They now appear with all the major companies of the world as guest artists. They have performed in the classics as well as modern works with great success and received much acclaim. Their dancing has revealed their beautiful classical training to which they acknowledge their indebtedness and which they claim is the finest in the world.

Denmark

The Royal Danish Ballet is an unique company for it retains many ballets from the Romantic period in its repertoire. This link with the nineteenth century comes from the legacy left by the great choreographer and teacher August Bournonville (1805–79).

Trained by his father, who was a leading dancer and the ballet master at the Theatre Royal, Copenhagen, Bournonville first appeared on stage at the age of twelve in a ballet by Vincenzo Galeotti (1733–1816). Later he went to Paris to study with Auguste Vestris and appeared in Paris and London before returning to Copenhagen in 1828. He was invited to become the leading dancer, choreographer and teacher, a vivid example of the versatility of the artists of the time. He was to produce over fifty ballets and his first great success was *La Sylphide* (1836) in which the title role was danced by his pupil, the seventeen-year-old Lucile Grahn. This ballet was based on that created by Filippo Taglioni for his daughter Marie, but Bournonville used different music and his own choreography. There was also more emphasis on the male role which he himself danced, maintaining the balance between the male and female roles. Bournonville did not allow the ballerina to become the dominating figure in any of his works, unlike other ballets of that time. It is a great tribute to him that *La Sylphide* remains in the repertoire of contemporary companies and is often performed today.

Other ballets soon followed, many of which incorporated national themes. After six months in Italy, Bournonville returned to produce the

50

very popular *Napoli*. Many famous Danish dancers made their débuts in this ballet as children.

Bournonville was a great teacher and his technique is still taught in the Royal Danish Ballet School today, enabling dancers to interpret his choreography with understanding and authenticity. It has also produced some great dancers with an unique quality and sensitivity, notably Erik Bruhn (1928–), one of Denmark's most famous dancers. Other outstanding figures are Toni Lander (1931–), Neils Kehlet (1938–), Peter Martins and Peter Schaufuss (1949–), all of whom have gained international fame. Bournonville expressed the fear that when he died his ballets would also become lost and forgotten. Time, however, has proved his fears unfounded and his works have been the Royal Danish Ballet's greatest inheritance. This was largely due to the work of one of his pupils, Hans Beck (1861–1952), who continued to teach the Bournonville method and faithfully preserve the ballets.

In 1979, the centenary of the death of Bournonville was marked by the presentation of several of his ballets including *The Conservatory* which is a work based on his studies with Auguste Vestris in Paris in the 1820s, and *Far From Denmark* which dates from 1860 and is an unique survival from the vaudeville ballet. Other works in this festival included *The Life Guards of Amager* and *Kermesse at Bruges*.

Critics, choreographers and dancers from all over the world attended the performances to honour Denmark's greatest artist in the world of dance.

The Royal Danish Ballet also still performs a ballet from the Vincenzo Galeotti period, *The Whims of Cupid and The Ballet Master* (1786), which is one of the oldest surviving ballets. Galeotti, an Italian, came to Copenhagen in 1775 as ballet master and remained in Denmark for the rest of his life. The ballet has been slightly revised since his time, but the amusing story of Cupid mixing up various couples reveals a wit that was appreciated in the eighteenth century.

In 1932 Harald Lander (1905–71) was appointed director of the company and he held this position until 1951 when he left to pursue a more international career. He was a former pupil of the Royal Danish School and had been taught by Beck; like his predecessors he became dancer, choreographer, teacher and director. He realised that the future of the company could not rest on the old ballets alone and during his administration he created over thirty works for the company, many using Danish composers. One of his most well-known ballets was *Etudes* which is now in the repertoire of many companies including the London Festival Ballet. Flemming Flindt (1936–   ), the Danish-trained dancer who became the director of the company, also followed this policy and choreographed such contemporary works as *The Lesson, The Triumph of Death* and *The Young Man Must Marry*, all based on plays by Eugene Ionesco and using Danish composers and designers. His most recent work is *Salome* which was presented by his own dancers in a circus ring, to music by the British composer Peter Maxwell-Davies.

Recently the company has been directed by Henning Kronstam (1934–   ), another dancer who has trained in the Danish School.

Many choreographers have produced ballets for the company and the company frequently tours overseas. It is acclaimed for its classical style as well as the presentation of the Bournonville works.

Germany

There are over sixty opera houses in West Germany, most of which support ballet companies. In some of the smaller towns the dancers perform mainly in operas and operettas with only occasional evenings of full ballet, but in the major cities such as Hamburg, Stuttgart, Düsseldorf, Frankfurt, Munich and West Berlin there are some very fine professional companies giving full ballet programmes.

In the eighteenth and nineteenth centuries many distinguished dancers and ballet masters worked in Germany, but unhappily this tradition did not continue. It was music and the opera which became predominant and it was only after World War II, when companies such as the Sadlers Wells Ballet, the Marquis de Cuevas Ballet and others started to tour, that an interest in ballet was re-created. Today, Germany employs more dancers than any other European country, excluding the Soviet Union.

One of the most outstanding companies is the Stuttgart Ballet which undertakes international tours with great success. Stuttgart has had a long association with dance and it is appropriate that a renowned company should emerge from that city. Noverre, the eighteenth-century innovator, was ballet master from 1759 to 1767 and it was here that he staged his most famous ballet, *Medée et Jason*. In 1824 Marie Taglioni appeared in Stuttgart in several ballets produced by her father, but it was only when the interest in ballet became widespread in Germany that Stuttgart began to develop again as a ballet centre.

In 1957 Nicholas Beriozoff (1906–   ) became ballet master and produced several of the Petipa and Fokine classics; basic works which are essential for the development of a company.

52

John Cranko, a brilliant South African choreographer working with the Royal Ballet in London, was invited in 1960 to produce, in Stuttgart, his ballet *The Prince of the Pagodas*, a work which he had mounted at Covent Garden. A year later, feeling the need for the challenge of working with another company, he accepted an invitation to become the director at Stuttgart. He held this post until his untimely death in 1973. Under his guidance the company became one of the most interesting of companies, and gained world eminence. Cranko possessed a great theatrical sense and created for the Stuttgart company a repertoire that covered short ballets without plots, amusing ballets and full-length works. He also maintained the classics, and with such a varied selection and large number of ballets, public interest was aroused both in Germany and worldwide. Cranko inspired the company with his work, and in particular, the Brazilian dancer Marcia Haydée whom he had discovered at the Royal Ballet School in London. Recognising her potential he developed her talents and she became a powerful and dramatic ballerina with a great gift for comedy. Some of Cranko's finest works were created for Haydée, such as *Romeo and Juliet*, *Onegin* and *The Taming of the Shrew*.

Since 1976 Haydée has guided the fortunes of the company and by following Cranko's policy has discovered and developed new talent, both with dancers and choreographers. Rosemary Helliwell (1955–), is a new and promising choreographer who has created several successful ballets for the company.

Kenneth MacMillan has been a frequent visitor to Stuttgart and in recent years has choreographed several works for the company. His ballet *Lied von der Erde*, or *Song of the Earth*, to a song cycle by Mahler was so successful that it was later re-produced for the Royal Ballet. One of his most impressive ballets was *Requiem*, danced to the music of Fauré's Requiem Mass; this has proved to be a wonderful tribute to the ability of the company.

Two of Stuttgart's outstanding male dancers who have given terrific support as well as brilliant interpretations of Cranko's ballets, are Richard Cragun (1944–) and Egon Madsen (1942–). The Stuttgart Ballet School plays an important part in developing new talent and Birgit Keil (1944–), who trained at the school, has become the first oustanding German ballerina.

An interesting reputation has been built up by the Hamburg Ballet. The present choreographer, American-born John Neumeier (1942–), who was previously at Frankfurt for three years, has created ballets which are original and theatrical. They include *Romeo and Juliet, Meyerbeer-Schumann, Mahler's Third Symphony, Illusions—Like Swan Lake* and *Petrushka Variations*. His works are much admired in Germany for the brilliant ideas and staging. He has also produced ballets for the National Ballet of Canada, the American Ballet Theatre, the Scottish Ballet and other companies.

Berlin's interest in dance dates back to 1742 when the opera house of the Duke of Brandenburg was opened. The ballet was managed by a series of French ballet masters until the middle of the nineteenth century, when Paul Taglioni (Marie's brother) directed the ballet for twenty-five years.

As a capital city Berlin played host to all the famous dancers of the time including Fanny Elssler and Marie Taglioni, as well as the Diaghilev Ballet and Isadora Duncan. Although a ballet company has always been maintained, a national company has never been established. The present Opera House, the Deutsche Oper, West Berlin, supports a large ballet company, and it was Tatiana Gsovsky (1901–   ) who had the greatest influence on twentieth-century ballet in the capital. During her nine years of residence as ballet mistress and choreographer her influence extended to the whole of Germany.

MacMillan was ballet master from 1966 to 1969, during which time he choreographed the ballet *Anastasia* for Lynn Seymour. This work was originally in one act but when it was produced in London for the Royal Ballet in 1971 he extended the theme and added two more acts.

The Berlin company does not travel much but one of their present ballerinas, Eva Evdokimova (1948–   ) has appeared as a guest artist with many companies and is frequently seen in London with the London Festival Ballet. Valery Panov and his wife Galina, two dancers who were allowed to leave the USSR are now with the company.

The company at Düsseldorf has much in common with the Stuttgart Ballet. Although it does not have the latter's international reputation, it does command a great respect for its work. This is largely due to the talented partnership of its ballet master, Erich Walter (1927–   ), and his designer, Heinrich Wendel (1915–   ). Their co-operation began in Wuppertal in 1953 and was to continue when Walter moved to the Deutsche Oper am Rhein, Düsseldorf. The interesting choreography of Walter combined with Wendel's designs plus the resources of the Opera House, led to the Düsseldorf Ballet becoming renowned for its productions. Most opera houses in Germany are frequently changing their ballet masters, but Walter has remained, and in his period of office has been able to build up a strong company, retaining and engaging better dancers and developing over the years, an overall style. His policy has been similar to that of Cranko at Stuttgart; he has separated the opera from the ballet with a small group dancing in opera productions. One of his leading male dancers Peter Breuer (1946–   ) has made many guest appearances with the London Festival Ballet as well as other companies.

The ballet companies in East Berlin and the German Democratic Republic tour mainly in Eastern Europe and have teaching methods and repertoires which stem from the USSR.

France

Paris has always been acknowledged as the artistic centre of Europe, and the Paris Opéra Ballet has a tradition that is unsurpassed by any other theatre in the world. The Paris Opéra has seen all the great dancers and it was here that the first performances of the ballets *La Sylphide* (1883), *Giselle* (1841), *Le Corsaire* (1856), *Coppélia* (1870) and *Sylvia* (1876) were given.

The great dancing masters of the seventeenth and eighteenth centuries all taught in the capital. Auguste Vestris, one of the key figures in the development of the classical ballet technique, remained at the Paris Opéra for thirty-five years and even partnered Taglioni there when he was seventy-five years old. Among Vestris's pupils were August Bournonville, Charles Didelot and Jules Perrot, all of whom were to take his teaching outside of France. Teachers in many parts of Europe would boast of being French trained as this gave them prestige and a final seal of approval.

By the early 1900s, in common with other European capitals, ballet had declined in popularity in Paris although a company was still maintained at the Opéra. This was the period of the *vieux abonnés*, when rich elderly gentlemen took season tickets for seats, which were usually in the front row of the stalls, in order to applaud their protégés. There was no genuine interest in the art of the ballet and the works themselves were merely vehicles in which ballerinas could be displayed surrounded by the *corps de ballet*. The painter, Edgar Degas (1834–1917), has immortalised the life and times of this period with his pictures of dancers.

Following the arrival of Diaghilev and his Ballet Russe in Paris in 1909 and with the appointment of Jacques Rouché as director at the Opéra in 1914, standards began to improve. Rouché, who was a great admirer of Diaghilev, was to direct the Opéra for the next thirty years, during which time he introduced many changes and slowly restored the ballet to its former eminence in the theatre. Following the principles of Diaghilev, he raised the standards of both designs and music. Under his directorship Fokine revised his *Daphnis and Chloë*, Pavlova appeared in *La Péri* and, in 1924, Olga Spessivtseva (1895–   ), a former Diaghilev ballerina and one of the most renowned dancers of her time, was engaged to dance in *Giselle*. This was the first step towards the establishment of a classical repertoire.

An extremely beautiful and very wealthy Russian dancer, Ida Rubinstein (1885–1960), formed a company in 1928 and presented lavish and spectacular productions using the finest designers, composers and choreographers of the day. Rubinstein had been chosen by Diaghilev to appear in his ballets of *Cléopàtre* and *Schéhérazade*, more for her beauty and acting ability than as a dancer. Her opulent company existed for several years and many of its young dancers, including Frederick Ashton, were later to become well-known figures in the ballet world.

Following the death of Diaghilev, his last male premier dancer, the Russian, Serge Lifar, was invited to become dancer and choreographer to the Paris Opéra. From 1930 until 1958 (apart from a brief period of absence) Lifar remained at the Opera House re-organising and establishing a company worthy of its tradition. One of his first reforms was to have the auditorium lights lowered during a performance. Formerly, part of the audience had been busily engaged looking at each other rather than at the stage. He also closed the Foyer de Danse, for it was here that the *vieux abonnés* met the ballet girls and many famous or infamous assignations were made. Needless to say, the changes met with great opposition and there were demands that the Cossack should be thrown out.

In his time at the Opéra, Lifar choreographed numerous ballets including the very popular *Noir et Blanc*, then called *Suite en Blanc*, and this ballet is still performed by the London Festival company today. He not only stimulated a wide interest in ballet, but also developed a new generation of French dancers. He concentrated especially on raising the standard of the male dancers and certainly set a good example by his own outstanding performances.

The first French ballerina to win international recognition was Yvette Chauviré (1917–   ). Beloved by Paris audiences, she was affectionately known as *La Chauviré nationale*. Other ballerinas to find fame at the Opéra were Lycette Darsonval (1912–   ), Nina Vyroubova

(1921–   ) and Liane Daydé (1932–   ).

Not only does the Paris Opéra have a long tradition of ballet but it also has a school which has supplied the company with dancers since it was first established in 1713. The French dancers are trained in a style which includes the best of both the French and Italian methods. The Italian ballerina and teacher, Carlotta Zambelli (1875–1968), who remained at the Opéra for over sixty years, had a great influence on the training. Her partner for many years, Albert Aveline (1883–1968), a French dancer, choreographer and teacher, re-vitalised the teaching of male dancers, as did Gustav Ricaux (1884–1961); they numbered Jean Babilée (1923–   ), Roland Petit (1924–   ) and Michael Renault (1927–   ) amongst their pupils.

The company has an unique method of promotion. Each year examinations are held and a dancer can only progress to a higher position within the company if the results are satisfactory. The first examination occurs at approximately fifteen years of age, after which comes entry into the *Quadrilles* of the *corps de ballet*. This is followed by entries into *Coryphées*, the *Sujets*, *Premier Danseurs* and *Première Danseuses*. The highest rank, only obtained by nomination, is *Etoile*, which is, of course, much coveted. The leading ballerinas and male dancers have all achieved this status. The list of étoiles include some of the finest French dancers. Ghislaine Thesmar (1943–   ) and Noelle Pontois (1943–   ) are two étoile ballerinas who have made many guest appearances with other companies, as has Patrice Bart (1945–   ) who was awarded the title in 1972.

Since Lifar's retirement, the company has had several directors including Harald Lander, the Danish choreographer. It is now run by the French ballerina Violette Verdy.

Following World War II a group of dancers from the Opéra felt the need to break away from the company and experiment with ballet. This was not unlike the move made by Fokine and his dancers at St. Petersburg, which resulted in the formation of Diaghilev's Ballet Russe. A company was formed which became known as Les Ballets des Champs Elysées. From the beginning it gained the interest of Jean Cocteau, Kochno and Christian Bérard, all outstanding figures in the arts world. The new company's ballets, music and décors were unique in their originality and beauty and, as with the Diaghilev company, made a great impression.

Janine Charrat (1924–   ) and Roland Petit both choreographed outstanding ballets for the company. Petit's *Le Jeune Homme et la Mort*, danced to the music of Bach, introduced jazz style movements in a contemporary setting, something quite unknown in 1946. One of the outstanding dancers in the company was Jean Babilée who created the role in *Le Jeune Homme* which brought him much acclaim.

In 1948 Petit left Les Ballets des Champs Elysées to form the Ballet de Paris. It was for this company that he created *Carmen* with its magnificent role for his wife, Renée Jeanmaire (1924–   ). Later she appeared in films, danced in a New York musical and appeared as a singer at the Casino de Paris, displaying an amazing range of talent which has made her a much beloved artist. In 1979 she gave an astonishing performance at the Opera House, Monte Carlo, in Petit's new ballet *La Chauve Souris*. Petit now directs the ballet in Marseilles and has choreographed ballets for many companies including the Royal Ballet and the Royal Danish Ballet.

Another company which did much to revive memories of the Ballet Russe days was the Grand Ballet du Marquis de Cuevas. This company travelled all over the world presenting ballets on a very lavish scale with dancers such as Vyroubova, Serge Golovine (1924–   ), Rosella Hightower (1920–   ) Georges Skibine (1920–   ) and Marjorie Tallchief (1927–   ). Financed by the Marquis, the company had difficulty in surviving after his death. In 1961 it eventually ended.

Throughout France there are many companies attached to City or Municipal theatres. One of the most popular and successful of these is the Ballet Theatre Contemporain, first formed in 1968 at Amiens under the patronage of the Ministry of Culture. The company is now based in Angers and the policy of its director, Jean-Albert Cartier and its choreographer Francoise Adret, is to present new ballets with original scores and designs and using the work of the most interesting of contemporary artists. The company makes frequent tours and often appears on television. With such an actively changing repertoire the problem always is to find new and original choreographic material. Their décors are always startling but a strong repertoire is necessary to maintain such a company.

From the time of its court ballets to the present day, France has always maintained a high standard in the choice of décor, composer and choreographer. The ballets and companies have not always been successful, but all have an artistic uniqueness which is peculiar to France.

Belgium

Although Belgium is a small country, it has three major ballet companies. In the south there is the Royal Ballet of Wallonie, in the north the Royal Ballet of Flanders, and, based in Brussels, the Ballet of the Twentieth Century, or Le Ballet du XXme Siècle. Both of the Royal companies are known throughout Europe owing to their appearances at Festivals and their tours, but Le Ballet du XXme Siècle has an international reputation.

This company is directed by Maurice Béjart (1927–), a French-trained dancer who gained experience with many European ballet companies. It is a large company and is especially strong in male dancers. Béjart's choreography has a vital contemporary approach and the productions have clever visual effects, properties, scenery and lighting. He is a great showman and does not hesitate to shock his audiences with special creations and unorthodox dancing performed by well-trained performers.

His company will often appear in large sports arenas or circus tents and he has brought ballet to a much wider audience who might not otherwise have seen it. His works have a great impact especially on the younger generation, from whom he receives much support, as well as an extensive following.

Béjart often draws from the Diaghilev/Stravinsky scene, although the themes may be changed and the choreography adapted to the technique of his dancers. Ballets such as *The Firebird*, *Rite of Spring*, *Petrushka*, and even Diaghilev's *Le Spectre de la Rose* are all re-worked for present day audiences. The Diaghilev influence is also evident in Béjart's treatment of the Nijinsky/Diaghilev relationship in his production of *Nijinsky, Clown of God*.

Part of the Béjart shock treatment is in the use of the music, in which he blends classic with modern, pop or percussion. In *Notre Faust* he used sections of J.S. Bach's B Minor Mass together with Argentine tangos and Goethe quotations spoken in French and German. He also choreographed Beethoven's Ninth Symphony and Berlioz's *Damnation de Faust*. More recently there has been *Dichterliebe* and *Life* which he created for the great dancer, Jean Babilée.

Béjart has always maintained an international company of exceptionally talented dancers. The male dancers predominate in much of his choreography and the Italian dancer, Paolo Bortoluzzi (1938–) gave some brilliant performances during the twelve years that he was with the company.

Daniel Lommel (1943–), a French-Belgian dancer, and Jorge Donn (1947–), from the Argentine, are particularly expressive exponents of Béjart's work. Maina Gielgud (1945–), an English dancer, appeared with the company from 1967 until 1971 after which she appeared as guest artist with numerous other companies. Suzanne Farrell from the New York City Ballet was another ballerina who spent four years with Béjart before returning to the States. Working with Le Ballet du XXme Siècle gives dancers an added strength and authority and the company can attract such personalities as Plisetskaya, Nureyev and Alonso as guest artists.

Béjart also has a school, Mudra, which gives both classical and modern training; the two techniques being essential for his choreography. The school is strictly for professional training; the girls are between fifteen and nineteen years of age and the boys from fifteen to twenty-one, and they are not admitted unless they are already proficient in both classical and modern techniques.

Béjart's works are always strongly criticised in the Press but his company attracts large and enthusiastic audiences wherever they perform.

Holland

It was not until after World War II that an interest developed in ballet in Holland. Eventually two major companies, the National Ballet and the Nederlands Dans Theater became firmly established.

Two small companies had been doing pioneering work for some years but in 1961 these amalgamated to become the Dutch National Ballet. Sonia Gaskell (1904–), a Russian-born dancer who had worked with Diaghilev's Ballet Russe, became the artistic director and under her guidance the company developed; classical ballets were performed side by side with new works and gradually a repertoire of exceptional interest was created.

From the beginning Gaskell encouraged young Dutch choreographers and one of the first to emerge was the talented Rudi van Dantzig (1933–), whose first ballet, *Night Island* (1955), was later revived for the contemporary Ballet Rambert. His first major work, which was to bring both him and the company a wider recognition, was *Monument for a Dead Boy*. His ballets have strong modern themes with human, social or emotional problems. He uses mainly modern music, often electronic, and his choreography is a blend of modern and the classical.

After Gaskell's retirement, van Dantzig was made artistic director of

1 Marie Taglioni (1804–84). The first of the Romantic ballerinas, shown here in her most famous role as the Sylph in *La Sylphide*. Lithograph coloured by hand by E. Morton after A. E. Chalon.

2 *La Sylphide.* The Royal Danish Ballet's production of this famous Bournonville
ballet, with Anna Laëkerson as the Sylph and Henning Kronstam as James.

3 *La Sylphide.* A scene from Act 1 with the Scottish Ballet.

4 *Giselle.* Mikhail Baryshnikov as Albrecht and Natalia Makarova as Giselle in Act 2 of the New York City Ballet's production.

5 *Giselle*. The Scottish Ballet in a scene from the greatest of the Romantic ballets.

6 *Napoli*. The popular Bournonville work performed by the Scottish Ballet, shown here in the *pas de six* from Act 3.

7 *La Fille Mal Gardée.* Ashton's masterly interpretation of the 18th-century theme. Nadia Potts and Tomas Schramek with the National Ballet of Canada.

8 *La Fille Mal Gardée.* David Blair as Colas and Merle Park as Lise in the Royal Ballet's production.

9 *The Sleeping Beauty*. Petipa's great classic with David Wall and Merle Park of the Royal Ballet.

10 *The Sleeping Beauty*. The Bluebird *pas de deux* with Mary Jago and Tomas Schramek of the National Ballet of Canada.

11 *Raymonda*. The Australian Ballet in a version by Nureyev after the original by Petipa.

12 *Raymonda*. Margot Fonteyn in the title role.

13 *Le Corsaire.* Natalia Makarova and Yuri Soloviev in the Kirov production.

14 *Don Quixote*. Fernando Bujones as Basilio with the American Ballet Theatre.

15 *Swan Lake*. The Royal Ballet production with Merle Park as Odette and Anthony Dowell as Prince Siegfried.

16 *The Nutcracker*. Rudolf Nureyev as Drosselmeyer in Act 1.

17 *The Nutcracker.* Peter Darrell's production of this ever-popular Christmas Ballet, with the Scottish Ballet.

18 *The Nutcracker*. Elaine McDonald of the Scottish Ballet in the Arabian Dance from the Kingdom of the Sweets.

19 *Coppélia*. Vanessa Harwood as Swanilda with the National Ballet of Canada.

20 *Coppélia*. Mikhail Baryshnikov and Alla Sizova in the Kirov's version of this popular ballet.

21 Adeline Genée (1878–1970). This celebrated Danish ballerina was the first dancer to be created a Dame of the British Empire.

22 *Les Sylphides*. The London Festival Ballet in Fokine's tribute to the Romantic era.

23 *Les Sylphides*. Jennifer Penney, David Wall and Lesley Collier in the Royal Ballet's version.

24 Bakst costume. This was designed for Nijinsky's role in *Le Dieu Bleu*.

25 *The Firebird.* One of Fokine's famous ballets, with David Wall and Antoinette Sibley of the Royal Ballet dancing the roles first created by Fokine and Karsavina in Diaghilev's Ballet Russe.

26 *Petrushka.* Derek Rencher as the Moor, Jennifer Penney as the Ballerina and Alexander Grant as Petrushka in the Royal Ballet's production.

27 *The Green Table.* Kurt Jooss's outstanding political satire danced by the CAPAB Ballet.

28 *The Green Table.* A scene from the CAPAB Ballet production with Eduard Greyling as Death and Ann Layfield as the Mother.

29 *Façade*. Frederick Ashton and Moira Shearer in the Tango from one of Ashton's wittiest ballets.

30 *Serenade*. Balanchine's ballet of pure dancing performed by the Dance Theatre of Harlem.

31 *The Rake's Progress*. The Royal Ballet in a work based on the Hogarth paintings and choreographed by de Valois.

32 *Checkmate*. A dramatic moment from de Valois' ballet with Maina Gielgud as the Black Queen.

33 *Checkmate*. Robert Helpmann as the Red King in the Royal Ballet production.

34 *Graduation Ball.* A very popular ballet choreographed by David Lichine and danced here by the London Festival Ballet.

35 *Enigma Variations.* Wayne Sleep in the Royal Ballet's tribute to Edward Elgar.

36 *Symphonic Variations*. Ashton's brilliant abstract work for six dancers performed by the Royal Ballet.

37 *Cinderella.* Frederick Ashton and Robert Helpmann as the Ugly Sisters. Their teamwork in this ballet has never been surpassed.

38 *Marguerite and Armand*. Margot Fonteyn and Rudolf Nureyev in one of the most loved of Ashton's ballets. The roles were created as a tribute to these two dancers.

39 *Afternoon of a Faun.* Antoinette Sibley and Anthony Dowell in the modern interpretation by Jerome Robbins of Nijinsky's *L'Apres-midi d'un Faune.*

40 *Romeo and Juliet.* The Stuttgart Ballet in John Cranko's version of Shakespeare's tragedy.

41 *Romeo and Juliet.* Merle Park as Juliet and Wayne Eagling as Romeo in Mac-Millan's interpretation for the Royal Ballet.

42 *Romeo and Juliet*. Rudolf Nureyev as Romeo in his own production for the London Festival Ballet.

43 *The Dream*. Lucette Aldous as Titania and Ronald Emblem as Bottom in the ballet devised by Ashton for Shakespeare's 400th anniversary.

44 *The Dream.* Vanessa Harwood and Tomas Schramek of the National Ballet of Canada. This very successful ballet is performed by many companies.

45 *The Rite of Spring.* Monica Mason of the Royal Ballet in MacMillan's version of the controversial Diaghilev/Nijinsky ballet.

46 *Spartacus*. A spectacular ballet from the Bolshoi company danced to the music of Khachaturian.

47 *Jazz Calendar*. Cynthia Anderson of the Joffrey Ballet in one of the many Ashton works performed by this company.

48 *Manon.* A scene from the Royal Ballet's production of MacMillan's ballet, with David Wall.

49 *Mayerling.* MacMillan's dramatic work for the Royal Ballet with Wendy Ellis and David Wall.

50 *A Month in the Country.* Lynn Seymour as Natalia and Anthony Dowell as Beliaev
in an Ashton ballet based on Turgenev's famous play.

51 *Nijinsky, Clown of God*. Suzanne Farrell and Jorge Donn of the Ballet of the 20th Century in a pose typical of Béjart's choreography.

52 *Nijinsky, Clown of God*. Farrell and Donn in this large scale work which endeavoured to give the reasons for Nijinsky's madness.

53 *The Tales of Hoffman.* The Scottish Ballet in a scene from Peter Darrell's work based on the opera.

54 *The Merry Widow.* The Australian Ballet in the first full-length work commissioned for the company.

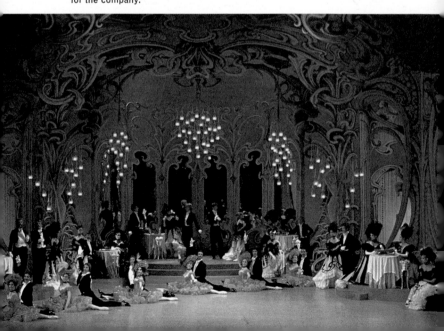

55 *The Tempest*. Lucy Burge and Mark Wraith in Glen Tetley's version of the Shake-speare play for the Ballet Rambert.

56 *For Those who Die as Cattle.* One of the modern works in the Ballet Rambert repertoire.

57 *Ursprung.* A contemporary ballet choreographed by Royston Muldoom and performed by the Scottish Ballet.

58 *Manifestations.* A very popular work from the **Dance Theatre of Harlem.**

59 *Polonaise*. One of the modern ballets performed by the London Contemporary Dance Theatre.

60 *Pierrot Lunaire*. An outstanding performance by Christopher Bruce of the Ballet Rambert, shown here with Lucy Burge, won him great acclaim.

61 *Push comes to Shove.* Baryshnikov in Twyla Tharp's brilliant and amusing work. This was the first role created for Baryshnikov in the West.

62 George Balanchine (right) at a rehearsal with Peter Martins of the New York City Ballet.

63 Alicia Markova rehearsing a dancer in *Les Sylphides*.

64 A boys' class at the Royal Ballet School.

the Dutch National and the company continued to go from strength to strength. Based in Amsterdam, the company tours widely and is greatly admired for the originality of its modern repertoire. In 1973 Hans van Manen (1932–), another interesting Dutch choreographer joined the National and was soon followed by a third, Toer van Schayk (1936–). With these three excellent choreographers, the company presented a wide range of interesting and often controversial ballets. All of these show a great influence from modern painting, sculpture and the cinema. In a recent ballet, *Live/Life*, van Manen choreographed the first part, *Live* and his two colleagues the second part, *Life*. In *Live* a television camera-man follows a dancer so that she can be seen on an immense screen in close-ups, or in actuality on stage. Action also takes place in the theatre foyer and corridors all of which can be followed by the audience. The principal dancer is eventually seen disappearing out of the theatre into the street and finally out of sight.

Nureyev frequently dances with the company and he created the central role in van Dantzig's *Blown in a Gentle Wind*. He also danced in *The Ropes of Time*, a ballet choreographed by van Dantzig for the Royal Ballet.

Van Manen has also choreographed for the Royal Ballet, with works such as *Four Schumann Pieces* and *Grosse Fuge*. A version of the ballet *L'Après-midi d'un Faune* has been re-choreographed by van Schayk and called *Faun*. In the original, a faun surprises a Greek nymph and steals one of her scarves. In the modern version, Nureyev danced as a porter in a factory and the encounter is with two girl machinists who leave their work to dance with him. Diaghilev might have approved but not Debussy!

With three such choreographers new ballets frequently appear both for the Dutch National and other companies.

Holland's other company, which is based in The Hague, is the Nederlands Dans Theater. At the beginning, new works based on either classical or modern techniques were presented, but gradually the modern style predominated and American dancers and choreographers began to work with the company. Glen Tetley began to influence the outlook and the policy of the company and van Manen from the National became one of the main choreographers. Both choreographers were much in demand and in 1971 both van Manen and Tetley withdrew from the company.

The Nederlands Dans Theater is a hard working company which produces about ten new ballets every year. Many of these are avant-garde

The combination of classic and modern technique shown by dancers of the Nederlands Dans Theater in November Steps, choreographed by Jiri Kylian.

with mixed media methods. One of its greatest successes has been *Carmina Burana*, which was choreographed by the American, John Butler (1920–). There have also been experiments combining dance films and live choreography simultaneously. It was one of the first companies to have nude sequences which have proved to be an acquisition of doubtful merit. The company is very strong with a team of excellent Dutch dancers as well as others from abroad. It is now directed by Jiri Kylian (1947–) and has become less experimental but has a more direct policy and outlook.

A small but valuable company is the Scapino Ballet. This was formed in 1945 by Hans Snoek (1906–) and is the oldest of Holland's companies. Its repertoire is designed to appeal to young people as well as to a more adult audience. This company has done much to develop an interest in ballet and has presented works and performances of a very high standard. Many of the Scapino dancers have graduated to the Dutch National Ballet. This company tours throughout Holland and is able to visit small towns where performances by larger companies would be impracticable. They have also carried out brief visits overseas.

Austria and Italy

In the eighteenth and nineteenth centuries both Austria and Italy were important centres of dance. In Italy, during the great Renaissance period when the arts flourished, the court ballets and dances influenced the rest of Europe.

Italy and Austria have been closely linked, especially in the nineteenth century when Italy was under the domination of the Austrian Empire. Choreographers such as Salvatore Viganò, divided their time between the two capitals. Viganò's greatest spectacles were performed at the Teatro all Scala in Milan, where, following the tradition of the Renaissance entertainments, he used the most elaborate and magnificent stage sets. His influence is still reflected in productions of both opera and ballet.

In 1812 a school was founded in association with La Scala and the great Carlo Blasis was appointed director in 1837. Even during the European decline in ballet, Italy still maintained the finest teaching traditions and it was from Italy that many famous virtuoso ballerinas emerged to appear in the capitals of Europe; dancers such as Legnani and Zambelli.

Italy has always been the centre of opera and during the decline in the popularity of ballet in Europe it replaced a dying art aided by the works of such composers as Bellini, Donizetti and Verdi. Ballet was included in the operas but only as a diversion to please the male members of the audience. Composers wrote beautiful music for the human voice but the music for the ballet was unbelievably trite. This meant that Italy and Austria became increasingly 'opera conscious', and have remained so until today.

Milan and Rome support large ballet companies but they unfortunately suffer from frequent changes of direction and repertoires. Both companies present the classic ballets as well as contemporary works by guest choreographers, but a lack of definite policy is evident.

Italy still trains some exceptional dancers who appear with other companies. Examples are, Carla Fracci (1936–), Liliana Cosi (1941–), Elisabetta Terabust (1946–) and the male dancer Paolo Bortoluzzi.

In Vienna, ballet has also suffered from a lack of definite direction and a bias towards opera. However it does have an interesting repertoire from such masters as Balanchine, Robbins, Cranko, Massine, Neumeier and van Manen. Although this company is not well known internationally, one of its leading male dancers, Karl Musil (1939–) has made many guest appearances with the London Festival Ballet and other companies.

Canada
Canada has, in a comparatively short time, developed an outstanding company, the National Ballet of Canada. In 1976 it celebrated its twenty-fifth anniversary, reminding the world of its growth and great accomplishments in this period.

The wish to form a national company in Canada was promoted by the Royal Ballet's tours of North America in 1949. To Ninette de Valois, the idea of a country as large as Canada without a national ballet company was unthinkable. She proposed that Celia Franca (1921–), a member of the Royal Ballet, should undertake the task of founding one. Franca was both artist and dancer, with experience as a ballet mistress, but in her mission in Canada she was faced with many problems and suffered many disappointments. Even when subsidised by the Canadian Council and the Ontario Arts Council, a ballet company is very expensive to maintain with its dancers, costumes and music. Also, in a country which is not strongly inclined towards an art such as ballet, there is not a great deal of sympathetic understanding.

From the beginning, Franca followed the de Valois policy, using classic ballets as a sound base for a repertoire and building on this

112

reliable foundation with works by modern choreographers. In 1964 Erik Bruhn mounted Bournonville's ballet *La Sylphide*, and this was followed two years later by his very controversial production of *Swan Lake*.

Nureyev has frequently appeared as a guest artist with the company as well as producing his version of *The Sleeping Beauty* with them. From Stuttgart came Cranko's *Romeo and Juliet* and from London came Ashton's *La Fille Mal Gardée*. Roland Petit has also choreographed ballets for the company as have Tudor and Neumeier. The company is now faced with the problem shared with many other companies, that of finding new choreographers. Workshops are held and new and interesting works are emerging, which indicate that in the future the company will have an original repertoire. It maintains a strong link with the Royal Ballet, and in 1976 Alexander Grant (1925–), an exceptionally brilliant character dancer from Covent Garden, was appointed artistic director.

There are two other companies in Canada, each having its own school and each working in a different way. Like the National Ballet, the Royal Winnipeg Ballet was founded by an Englishwoman, Lancashire-born Gweneth Lloyd (1901–). This company has the distinction of being the oldest of the Canadian companies and the first in the British Commonwealth to be given a Royal Charter; this was granted by Queen Elizabeth II in 1953. The company has travelled extensively and is smaller in size than the National, having only about twenty-five dancers. The relationship between the two companies is similar to that between the Royal Ballet and the Ballet Rambert, where the smaller company concentrates on one-act ballets and the larger one on the classics.

In 1958 the Canadian dancer and teacher, Arnold Spohr took over the direction of the Royal Winnipeg Ballet, and has guided the company through a series of near disasters and financial crises. Touring in Canada is expensive because of the huge distances to be covered. New ballets can be a drain on resources and the company supports a large repertoire which has been built up over the years. The ballets are very varied, some provocative, others bizarre but a bad season or an indifferent ballet can bring a dramatic debit to a small budget.

The company dances with zest and attack which endears them to the public. Although they present one or two classical items they are not a classically oriented company and rely largely on contemporary choreographers. Brian Macdonald (1928–) choreographed ballets such as

Karen Kain, the National Ballet of Canada's leading ballerina, as Juliet in Cranko's version of Romeo and Juliet.

Les Whoops de Doo and *Aimez Vous Bach*. Agnes de Mille choreographed several new works such as *The Rehearsal* and *Bitter Weird*, as well as old favourites such as *Rodeo* and *Fall River Legend*. They also dance a ballet called *Ecstasy of Rita Joe* which was commissioned by the Manitoba Indian Brotherhood. Neumeier produced *The Nutcracker* and Oscar Araiz (1940–   ), the Argentinian dancer and choreographer, contributed a challenging and provocative interpretation of *Rite of Spring*.

Canada's third company is Les Grands Ballets Canadiens, which is based in Montreal. This developed from a group of television dancers in 1956 and now performs such classics as *Giselle* and *Swan Lake* as well as more modern works. One of its most successful ballets has been *Tommy* by Fernand Nault (1921–   ), choreographed to a 'rock' opera by the British pop group, The Who. In 1974 Macdonald was appointed artistic director, and his aims have been to make the company a vehicle for new Canadian talent embracing music and design.

In a country as large as Canada the smaller companies presenting ballets have a particular value, as their existence emphasises the growth and interest developing in ballet as an art, as well as developing an audience for the home based and visiting companies.

The Canadian standard of teaching is very high and many dancers have achieved success outside their own country. Lynn Seymour, the brilliant ballerina who has had an outstanding success with the Royal Ballet in London, was born in Alberta and first studied dance in Vancouver. Jennifer Penney (1946–   ) from Vancouver and Wayne Eagling (1950–   ) from Montreal are two other outstanding Canadian dancers who are now with the Royal Ballet in London.

Australia

During the 1920s and 1930s Pavlova, Genée and the de Basil Ballet Russe de Monte Carlo toured Australia and brought ballet to audiences far from Western culture. An interest was created but it was the driving force of Edouard Borovansky (1902–59), a former Ballet Russe dancer, which did much to keep that interest alive. He was a Czech dancer and choreographer and with the aid of his wife he opened a school in Melbourne in 1939 and several years later formed the Borovansky Ballet. It was not easy to support a ballet company in the vastness of Australia especially at a time when grants were non-existent. The distances to be travelled were daunting; to travel from Sydney to Perth is the equivalent in distance to travelling across Europe from Britain to Greece. In

115

spite of this handicap Borovansky kept the company performing throughout the 1940s into the 1950s, and right up to the time of his death.

Teachers throughout Australia began to develop a growing interest in dance and gradually a new generation of dancers and choreographers developed. A new company was urgently required and in 1962 the Australian Ballet, with several Borovansky members in it, was founded. Peggy van Praagh (1910–), a former dancer and teacher, was appointed director. She had been assistant director of the Sadlers Wells Theatre Ballet for several years and was an excellent teacher. In the 1930s when the ballet was developing in England, she had created roles in the Tudor ballets *Dark Elegies* and *Jardin Aux Lilas*, and she had a thorough knowledge of ballet from all aspects. Under her guidance the Australian Ballet began to develop and soon established itself as a strong company. The first performance was given in Sydney in 1962 with Sonia Arova (1927–) and Erik Bruhn dancing in *Swan Lake*. The Australian principals were Marilyn Jones (1940–), who was to make guest appearances with the London Festival Ballet; Kathleen Gorham (1932–), who had previously danced with the Sadlers Wells company, the Ballet de Paris and the du Cuevas company; and Garth Welch (1939–) a fine danseur noble.

Ballets by Ashton, Balanchine and Cranko were presented and in 1964 Robert Helpmann was invited to choreograph an all Australian ballet, *The Display*. Helpmann was appointed director when Peggy van Praagh retired in 1974. During his term of office he was to contribute several ballets, all with the strong theatrical flair for which he was noted. Examples are the ballets *Yugen* and *Sun Music*. Helpmann is one of Australia's greatest personalities. Born in Mount Gambier, he first experienced ballet at the age of sixteen when he saw Pavlova dance in Melbourne. He joined her company for the rest of her tour becoming a student member, taking daily classes with Novikov and performing small parts.

Several years later he was persuaded to go to London by his friend Margaret Rawlings the brilliant actress. He joined the Vic-Wells Ballet and remained with the company for many years forming a great partnership with Fonteyn. A true man of the theatre he possessed a great talent which embraced both dance and drama.

Robert Helpmann became one of Australia's greatest contributors to British ballet.

Petit, MacMillan, Tetley and Butler have all staged ballets for the

116

Australian company and Nureyev has produced new versions of the Petipa works *Raymonda* and *Don Quixote*; the success of the latter resulted in it being filmed. Ronald Hynd choreographed and Helpmann produced a balletic version of *The Merry Widow* in which Margot Fonteyn danced the leading role on many occasions. The repertoire of this company is being constantly expanded, and recently, the Soviet ballet *Spartacus* was introduced. In 1979 André Prokovsky (1939–) choreographed a three-act version of Tolstoy's *Anna Karenina* with Galina Samsova (1937–) as guest artist dancing the role of Anna.

As with every large company a school is of the utmost importance and the Australian Ballet School, based in Melbourne, was established in 1964. It is directed by Margaret Scott (1927–), a Ballet Rambert dancer who settled in Australia following the tour of the Ballet Rambert in 1947–48.

The school has produced some strong technical dancers who are noted for their capacity for hard work. Many have gained prominence both at home and overseas. Marilyn Rowe (1946–), Gary Norman (1951–), Kelvin Coe (1946–) are all principals with the present company. John Meehan (1950–), a former principal, is now with the American Ballet Theatre.

Many Australian dancers have sought experience by dancing with European companies and then returned home. In ballet companies throughout the world Australian dancers can be found. Their work has revealed the excellence of their training and their ability.

Lucette Aldous (1939–), although born in New Zealand, studied in Sydney before joining the Royal Ballet School in London in 1955. She worked as a ballerina with the Ballet Rambert, the London Festival Ballet and the Royal Ballet before returning to lead the Australian Ballet. She now teaches at the School.

Elaine Fifield (1930–) was another Australian dancer who possessed exceptional talent. She went to England with a scholarship to the Royal Academy of Dancing and became first a soloist and then a ballerina at Covent Garden. In 1964 she returned home to the Australian Ballet and danced with them for several years.

British dancers also enjoy working in Australia. Recently Ann Jenner (1944–), a ballerina from the Royal Ballet, joined the Australian Ballet and achieved a great success with her interpretation of Lise in *La Fille Mal Gardée*.

New choreographers are also emerging, and from the workshop productions several ballets have been added to the repertoire, such as

Othello, by Welch, *Night Episode* by Meehan and Julia Cotton's *Super Man*.

The company has made many successful overseas tours and it has been admired for its attack and vigour. Former ballerina Marilyn Rowe is now the artistic director.

Other companies have developed in Australia and several of these are directed by ex-dancers who have gained experience in Europe and are now passing on their knowledge to a new generation.

The Queensland Ballet is directed by the Australian Harry Haythorne (1926–), a character dancer who had worked for several years in Britain.

The West Australian Ballet is based in Perth and is directed by Robin Haigh (1937–), a former Royal Ballet dancer who is also Australian.

There are numerous smaller groups who work either on a professional basis or as amateurs. Although they may not achieve international status they present ballets with a high standard of performance. The New South Wales Ballet Concert is a group which visits small towns and schools. Many other groups undertake exhausting tours which all help to stimulate the growing interest in ballet in this vast country.

Modern dance also has a wide following and Australian composers and designers are finding an outlet for their talents. Graeme Murphy is one of the most imaginative of choreographers working in the contemporary field and is the director of the progressive Sydney Dance Company.

Another important group is the Australian Dance Theatre which is based in Adelaide and is directed by English-born Jonathan Taylor (1941–). Taylor was for many years principal dancer with the Ballet Rambert and he has also choreographed several successful ballets for that company.

South Africa

The number of dancers and choreographers who come from South Africa is indeed impressive. The standard of teaching in that country has produced some very fine artists who have made important contributions to the ballet world. Maude Lloyd, the Cape Town dancer who was trained by Helen Webb, was one of the first to come to England. She joined the Ballet Rambert in 1927 and created many roles in the Ashton, Howard and Tudor ballets. Her beautiful classical line and quality of movement was much admired, and helped in establishing ballet.

118

Frank Staff, a very talented choreographer, was born in Kimberley and produced many ballets for South African companies as well as the Ballet Rambert. Nadia Nerina (1927–   ) from Cape Town, became one of the most brilliant ballerinas in the Royal Ballet. She created the role of Lise in Ashton's *La Fille Mal Gardée* which brought her international fame.

John Cranko, who had studied at the Cape Town University Ballet School, developed into a brilliant choreographer whose ballets are now danced by many companies including those in Canada, Australia, Stuttgart and London.

One of Ninette de Valois's policies was to include Commonwealth dancers in her company: dancers such as Alexis Rassine, David Poole, Patricia Miller, Maryon Lane, Desmond Doyle, Johaar Mosaval and, more recently, Phyllis Spira, Monica Mason, Deanne Bergsma, Vergie Derman, Margaret Barbieri and Vyvyan Lorrayne are all South African dancers who became members of the Royal or Sadlers Wells Ballet.

In a different field of dance Juliet Prowse (1937–   ) has had a great success in musicals, films and other forms of commercial entertainment. Classically trained, she grew too tall for ballet and specialised in modern work.

The exodus of dancers from South Africa was due to the lack of permanent professional companies. However, the Republic now supports two companies: the CAPAB, based in Cape Town, and PACT, which is in Johannesburg. Both companies operate on a full-time basis with a large number of dancers in each company.

The CAPAB (Cape Performing Arts Board) Ballet developed from a small company which was first started by Dulcie Howes (1908–   ), a South African who was a former dancer with the Pavlova company. In 1930 she returned to her native country to teach, and a few years later her school became part of the University of Cape Town. From this beginning the University of Cape Town Ballet started and became the first ballet company in South Africa. As with all pioneer companies, there were many problems, not the least being the constant loss of dancers to companies overseas. In 1965 the company became fully professional and changed its title to CAPAB. Permanent employment is now offered to over sixty dancers and although some still do leave, many return. When Howes retired in 1969 David Poole (1925–   ) was appointed as director. He had been a pupil of Howes and a Royal Ballet principal. Having gained a great deal of experience both in England and South Africa, he was well aware of the difficulties involved in running a company.

In Johannesburg the problems were similar to those in Cape Town. Several groups had been formed but the lack of financial assistance and the distances that had to be travelled gave no stability. In 1963 the PACT Ballet (Performing Arts Council, Transvaal) was created from a nucleus of dancers from the Johannesburg City Ballet, then directed by Faith de Villiers. The PACT Ballet became a strong and viable company and is now directed by the South African dancer Louis Godfrey (1930–) who has been a soloist and principal with the London Festival Ballet for over fourteen years. His co-director is his wife, Denise Schultze (1933–), a former PACT ballerina.

Both the South African companies present the classics as well as works by guest choreographers, and the two National schools supply trained dancers of a very high standard. They are fortunate in having theatres such as the Civic in Johannesburg and the Nico Malan in Cape Town, the latter being one of the best equipped theatres in the world. The support given by the government enables a large number of dancers to be employed and they tour extensively in the Republic. Smaller groups of dancers give special programmes in the more remote regions.

New Zealand

In 1978 the New Zealand Ballet celebrated its Silver Jubilee with a production of *The Sleeping Beauty*. During its twenty-five years of existence, the company has performed throughout the country, appearing in schools, small towns and the major cities.

The founder of the company was Poul Gnatt (1923–), a Danish dancer who first visited New Zealand when touring with the Borovansky Ballet in 1952. He saw the need for a professional company and returned to New Zealand in the following year to form what was to become the basis of the National Ballet. The company gave its first performance in June 1953.

The beginnings of a ballet company are always fraught with difficulties and during the formative years the dancers and the company suffered many hardships, both financial and physical, but courage and determination allowed them to survive. Gnatt also formed a 'Friends of the Ballet' (similar in pattern to that of the Royal Opera House, Covent Garden and the London Festival Ballet) which continues to flourish and give loyal support to the company.

In 1959, after six years in which Gnatt had fulfilled the artistic and administrative duties of the company, a directorate was formed which then became a Trust Board. Government funds, much sought after for many years, became a reality and with a sounder financial basis changes took place which enabled the company to develop.

The company seldom tours overseas, as distances and the cost of transportation makes it impracticable. The population of New Zealand is comparatively small but there is a strong and enthusiastic interest shown in dance.

Restricted to their own country the company requires an ever-changing repertoire. Apart from the classics, they have presented Ashton's *Façade* and *Les Patineurs*, Cranko's *Pineapple Poll*, Balanchine's *Serenade* and *Concerto*, as well as ballets with a more contemporary approach. To celebrate the Bournonville centenary, a production of *La Sylphide* was mounted.

As always, dancers have felt the need to gain more experience outside of their own country, and many have been successful in dancing with companies in Europe. This inevitably leads to a drain on the company, although vacancies are always eagerly sought by the students of the National Ballet School.

The quality of teaching in New Zealand is very good and dancers achieve a very high technical standard. Dancers will return to the company and give guest appearances, mount ballets or direct the company. Invaluable help and assistance has been given by Rowena Jackson, a former Royal Ballet ballerina together with her husband Philip Chatfield who is also a principal from the Royal Ballet. Sara Neil, who with her husband Walter Trevor, now teaches at the Royal Ballet School, Bryan Ashbridge, a former Royal Ballet soloist, Russell Kerr and Alexander Grant, who now directs the National Ballet of Canada are other prominent dancers who have supported the company. The mainstay of the company for many years has been Jon Trimmer, the leading male dancer, an ideal partner who gives strength and stability to his colleagues.

Other Countries

The national companies in Eastern Europe, including the Baltic Republics, Czechoslovakia, Poland, Hungary, Romania, Bulgaria and Yugoslavia are rarely seen in Western Europe. Their schools and training follow the USSR pattern, and many of the ballets that they produce are based on Soviet productions. The companies tour mainly within the Eastern bloc and visit overseas countries with similar political views. The ballets are well presented, and the dancers, as would be expected from their Russian training, are very good. Many of the cities still maintain opera houses from a past decade and others have more modern ones.

Bulgaria is known for its International Ballet Competition, which takes place at Varna, the Black Sea coastal resort. First held in 1964, the gold medals that are awarded are as prized in the ballet world as Olympic awards. Many famous ballet names have been recipients, including the Soviet dancers Vasiliev, Sizova, Makarova, Maximova, Laurovsky, Baryshnikov, Bessmertnova and Galina Panov (then known as Ragosina), as well as the brilliant Japanese dancers Hideo Fukagawa and Yoko Morishita, the London Festival ballerina Eva Evdokimova, and the American male dancer Fernando Bujones.

Many former dancers have guided the destinies of various companies throughout the world. The Cuban National Ballet is directed by the former ballerina from the American Ballet Theatre, Alicia Alonso. The British dancer and former Royal Ballet principal Brenda Last (1938–   ) now directs the ballet in Norway. Ninette de Valois, apart from her commitments with the two Royal companies and the Royal Ballet School, was invited in 1947 to form a school in Istanbul. With her able interest over the years, a strong company developed which is now based in Ankara. They produce ballets from the Royal Ballet repertoire and many dancers from Turkey have studied at the Royal Ballet School.

The growth of ballet in Japan in the last few years has led to the founding of numerous schools and dance companies. The main company is the Tokyo Ballet which has seventy-five members. Their repertoire is mainly based on the classics together with some later Soviet works. With their capacity for hard work, the Japanese have achieved a very high standard of technique and performance in a very short time.

The main dance centres of the world, London, Paris and New York, are frequently visited by overseas companies and their performances always create a widespread interest. In spite of vast distances all members of the ballet world remain closely linked.

5
The Training of a Dancer

Thousands of children, teenagers, adults and athletes enrol each year for ballet classes. Ballet is one of the most popular forms of dance and many begin to learn inspired by the beautiful classical line, the complete poise and the balance and co-ordination of a dancer. The adult approaches ballet to develop some of these qualities and to improve posture. The athlete needs the flexibility, rhythm and co-ordination. Children are fascinated by the fairy tale glamour and beauty and although some may never have seen a ballet performance, they are inwardly drawn to this type of dance. There is a perfection in a body which moves with disciplined control and grace.

Some people come to ballet classes on medical advice in order to develop limbs, correct spinal faults and for better breathing. For others it is a form of relaxation and is performed purely for pleasure. With those that have a more serious approach and possibly with a ballet career in view, it is more difficult. Of all the boys and girls who take up ballet, the percentage of success is small. A dancer's training is long and arduous and demands complete dedication.

Many children from three years of age onwards attend classes. These classes are designed to give them enjoyment and teach them to move expressively to music as well as to strengthen their muscles. At the age of six or seven they may take a Primary examination and then a year later take a First Grade. This is the beginning of a long training if seriously pursued.

For a child that has not danced before, the training should start at about eight years of age but not later than ten or twelve. There are exceptions when children have started later and have become successful dancers, but a later start is, on the whole, not advisable. For boys the commencing age can be later but ideally not after fourteen. Again there have been exceptions where late starters have become well known. Nureyev joined the Kirov School at the age of seventeen but he had had some folk dance experience as well as some ballet lessons before then.

It may be asked why ballet training should take so long. The answer lies in the fact that the body is developed very gradually and carefully through a series of well-constructed scientific exercises. The exercises are designed to give flexibility and strength to the muscles, enabling the dancer to jump, turn, beat, all with perfect grace, balance and control. The beautiful classical line of the dancer's leg is obtained by what is termed *turn-out*. To develop turn-out takes time: basically it consists of turning the leg in the hip socket.

Ballet cannot be forced, it must progress slowly and carefully. There are different levels and grades of examinations that have to be faced, all of which present new difficulties and challenges.

Attached to most national and major ballet companies there are schools which accept promising pupils. Some of these schools offer boarding and educational facilities together with dance study. Other schools are non-residential and offer training after normal school hours.

In England, the Royal Ballet School combines education with dance at the Junior School at White Lodge. Boys and girls of exceptional talent, who have had training elsewhere and who have a good academic standard, can apply to join the Senior School.

The English pattern of training, with slight variations, is followed in Denmark by the Royal Danish Ballet, as well as other countries.

In the USSR the two major schools are the Kirov Ballet School in Leningrad and the Bolshoi in Moscow. Acceptance into the schools is by audition and although thousands apply, very few are accepted. For the Kirov only twenty gain admittance out of countless applications from all over the USSR.

In England, preliminary auditions for the Royal Ballet School are held all over the country, followed by auditions in London. Parents are often unable to accept the limitations of their children and usually cannot appreciate the attributes needed for their children to succeed. Doctors and ballet specialists examine the children accepted to determine their health and lung capacity. They look for a compact body, well-proportioned limbs and a natural rotation of the hip. Correction of posture and poise as well as spinal faults is essential. The eventual height is important and can be estimated by special tests. For a girl, 5 ft 6 in (1.68 m) is the limit, although there have been exceptions when girls have grown beyond this height and still made successful careers.

Applicants are also examined for their musicality, an important asset for a dancer. The education of pupils must never be neglected and a certain academic standard is required and maintained. This is essential, as should the career as a dancer be interrupted for any reason such as health or injury, an educational background remains to allow for an alternative career.

The dedication of an applicant in future years cannot be over-estimated. Patience, imagination and humility are necessary and only time can prove if these qualities remain.

Non-acceptance by a national or major school does not necessarily rule out the prospect of a dancing career. There are, in England, various boarding schools of note which give an excellent education and dance training. There are also recognised dance training colleges with three-year courses for senior students.

Sadly, many children are turned down at auditions because of poor basic training which, if it has progressed too far, leaves irreparable damage. Poor teaching can result in bad posture, extended rib cage, hollow back, weak ankles causing a rolling of the feet or damaged feet from incorrect shoes or early pointe work. The choice of school is very important and the teachers should belong to a reputable dance organisation or society.

For girls, a moment arrives in their training when pointe work commences. This is a rising on the toes in special blocked shoes and should only be done under supervision and with great care. Pointe work is usually introduced at about twelve years of age although it depends on how much previous training has been done. Obviously a beginner at the age of twelve would not undertake pointe work immediately. Pointe work is only attempted after several years of training when the feet, legs and body are very strong. It commences gradually with simple rises; there are many dangers in starting too soon and feet can be damaged for life unless care is taken. In some countries teachers will put very young children on to pointe at a very early age and even after only a few lessons. This is really quite criminal. In England, as a precaution, manufacturers of ballet shoes do not make pointe shoes in very small sizes, which helps to prevent this practice.

As a dancer's training progresses, the technical side becomes more demanding. What has been one or two classes a week, each of an hour's duration, has to be extended into classes every day or at least several times weekly. At professional schools dancers take one or two classes a day as, at a certain stage, senior level examinations require a great deal of work if they are to be passed successfully. Unhappily, these added demands coincide with those made by other school examinations requiring time for study. It is at this point that many students discover that they do not possess the dedication that ballet demands or, possibly, there is a lack of stamina or a faulty figure. Altogether there can be a wide withdrawal from serious ballet training.

Many of the students that take up ballet do not necessarily intend to become professional dancers. For many it is a source of enjoyment or satisfaction together with the joy of a well-trained body.

According to USA statistics, it is estimated that only one out of ten thousand ballet students is accepted by a professional company. Those without professional ambitions support their local dance studios by performing in recitals or amateur productions and their training can be used in other ways.

Children who are accepted by a professional school do not always sustain the standard required. To be asked to leave is difficult for both parents and child to understand. It is hard to appreciate that even a slight imperfection can prevent a successful career in a profession which demands perfection. If a child is dedicated, a rejection is hard to accept. At such a time some will reject dance altogether but others will seek alternative schools or local studios and there are numerous dancers now working in both modern and classical fields that at one time did not reach the standard demanded of them. If the will is really present, they will continue come what may.

Marie Rambert was once asked by a student 'Do you think, Madam, that I will ever become a dancer?' She replied 'You have already answered yourself'. A dancer must never have doubts but must be prepared to spend the rest of his or her career working and perfecting.

Every professional commences a working day with a ballet class. Under the critical eye of a teacher, a period of an hour and a half will be spent stretching and flexing the muscles. This will be followed by rehearsals, costume fittings, understudy calls or special coaching. There is also a half-hour warm-up before a show commences.

Dancers will say 'If I don't take a class for a day I know it. If I don't take a class for two days my teacher will know it. If I don't take a class for three days the public will know it.' For a professional dancer the daily class is a ritual.

With the growth in the popularity of ballet and the much publicised careers of some of the world's greatest male dancers, more boys are now learning to dance. The image of the male dancer has changed considerably over the past twenty years. It is no longer considered as an unsuitable career and parents are more tolerant in their outlook when sons express the wish to become dancers.

In most dance schools boys and girls are trained together in their junior years and then divide into separate classes once the basic training has been given. Boys tend to work at a slightly slower pace than girls and have exercises to increase their elevation, beats and turns. They are also introduced to *pas de deux* in which they learn to support and lift their partners. Boys need to work in a class with other boys until their technique is firmly established.

What is a class? The dancers are dressed in tights, leg warmers, tunics and cross-over jumpers and arrive a few minutes before the commencement in order to gently flex their legs. In a professional class the dancers tend to wear a variety of practice clothes but for the student, clean tights, correct leotards, tunics or shirts for the men are expected. Girls have to dress their hair correctly and tie their shoes in the correct manner, all of which is part of the discipline required by ballet.

From the moment that a pupil joins a ballet class there has to be conformity. The class begins with a series of exercises in which the dancers hold on to a *barre*, or handrail, fixed to the studio wall. Companies when on tour travel with portable barres which can be used on the stage. Holding the barre with one hand, there is a series of exercises which warm and prepare the muscles of the body. The first exercise is always a series of *pliés* or bending movements of the knees and this exercise is a fundamental movement of all dancing. This is followed by exercises for the feet and legs combining tension, stretch and relaxation. Each exercise is executed first using one leg, then turning round and, with the other hand holding the barre, using the other leg. Barre work at major or professional level can take from twenty to thirty minutes, varying with the wishes of the teacher. The dancers then leave the barre and arrange themselves in rows in the centre of the room. At one time precedence was given to the principals of the company or the teacher's favourite pupils. A wayward pupil would be placed in the front row to get the full benefit of a barrage of words from the teacher and to remain under the gimlet eye.

It was not unknown for some maestros to carry a little stick or cane and to give an offending limb a far from gentle tap! The exercises in the middle of the room are known as centre practice or *exercises au milieu* and consist of a series of movements similar to those performed at the barre but now executed without support. They develop perfect balance and help sustain the turn-out without assistance from the barre.

Then follows *port de bras* or carriage of the arms. Dancers must learn to use their arms and hands just as much as their legs and feet. The *port de bras* exercises develop co-ordination of head and arms. *Adage* now

127

A class of thirteen-year-old girls at the Royal Ballet School, London, demonstrating port de bras.

follows and this consists of slow, sustained movements which help the dancer to develop balance, strength and co-ordination of movement and line. This helps also to prepare for *pas de deux*. The class ends with the *allegro* section which incorporates firstly quick jumps and beats which are followed by larger and more sustained jumps. Girls will change their shoes for pointe shoes ready for a series of special steps executed on pointe. The men perform some more spectacular jumps, *tour en l'air*, beats and *pirouettes*.

All the steps in ballet have French names and come from the period when the first Academy of Dance was founded in France. Ballet has an universal language and the French terms are used in every country. The execution of the steps may differ slightly according to the method of teaching, but a dancer can follow a class in any part of the world. A teacher may show a series of steps and say *'demi contretemps to croisé, assemblé dessus en face, bras en couronne, deux sissones fermées, ouverte en arrière'*, etc. (part of a set allegro in the Elementary syllabus of the Imperial Society of Teachers of Dancing (ISTD), Imperial Ballet Branch) and a well-trained dancer could follow. The various steps are used in the same way as words are used in a sentence and called *enchaînement* and executed by the dancer. Beginners will learn an *enchaînement* of perhaps two or more steps and gradually the mind and body are taught to maintain a series of steps. As an actor will learn a part in a play, dancers can learn and retain the steps of several ballets.

Each step in ballet combines two or more of the basic ways of moving of which there are seven. These are:

Plier—to bend: from which is derived the word *Plié*

Etendre—to stretch: from which is derived *Tendu* or *Tendue*

Relever—to rise: from which is derived *Relevé*

Sauter—to jump (also *Jeter*): from which comes *Sauté-Jeté*

Glisser—to glide (also *Chasser*): from which comes *Glissade-chasse*

Elancer—to dart: from which comes *Elance*

Tourner—to turn: from which comes *Tour* or *Tourne*.

Over the years the training and the shapes of the dancers have changed. In the Romantic period of the late nineteenth century, the long ballet skirt and the cut of the bodice influenced the movements of the dancers. The focal point was centred on the lower leg with the expressive use of head, arms and the shoulders. Class work stressed neat, exact and very strong foot work together with beautiful *port de bras* and mobility in the upper back. The lower rather than the whole leg was used.

129

The long ballet skirt became progressively shorter and was to become the tutu as used in the Petipa ballets. This gave the dancer more freedom in using her legs. The Italian-trained ballerinas were to thrill Russia and the rest of Europe by their virtuosity and technique. To exact footwork was added more extension of the leg, more strength to enable the dancer to sustain turns and balances.

Ballerinas tended to be short and compact. Olga Preobrazhenska (1870–1962), the Russian ballerina who later became a famous teacher in Paris, was tiny, as was Genée, but they both had very strong legs. Ninette de Valois commented at a lecture given at a Congress of the ISTD that 'present day dancers find it difficult to dance the Diaghilev ballets as they were based on personalities rather than the physical shape of the ballerinas. Diaghilev dancers would find it equally difficult to fit into our contemporary works'.

The present day tutu is worn very short and in modern works it is often replaced by leotards and all-over body tights. This has placed the accent on the whole body as well as its shape and the use of the limbs. This freedom of line has brought considerable changes. Dancers are required to have much greater mobility in the hip joint to enable them to lift legs higher. In training the emphasis has shifted with concentration on the use and height of the legs. The all-revealing costumes also demand good physiques: a girl short in the leg or big in the thigh does not look right in all-over tights and is consequently out of place with a professional company. At auditions great stress is laid on physique and a child with long, well-proportioned legs will have much more chance of acceptance.

Compared to the female, the male dancer has faced less change. He can jump higher and turn quicker. With the coming of unisex and the Jet Age, the roles of male and female have become less strongly defined. Men have developed higher leg lines and the once bulky thighs have disappeared. In some of the modern works where both sexes are dressed in similar costumes, it is hard to differentiate between the genders!

Dance is quick to reflect the age of which it is a part and none so much as in the contemporary scene. However, the classical ballets and training still remain the firm background and from this a dancer can approach any form of dance.

6
Going to the Ballet

The first introduction to any of the arts can be difficult, as personal choice or preference is variable. A ballet with a story is possibly the best choice as an introduction to this form of theatre. Many people have come to enjoy ballet through the classical works. These contain a story, are spectacularly presented and are, in general, what everyone imagines a ballet to be. Reactions vary as do the needs of the public. Some find a story distracting or miss the verbal communication; others find it too escapist or prefer ballet with a realistic approach. Ballets in which the dancers interpret the music and create expressive dance qualities, patterns and designs are very popular. Most companies have works of this type in their repertoire, for example, Ashton's *Symphonic Variations*, Robbins's *Dances at a Gathering* are two ballets which are pure dance, no messages, dramas or intrigues to work out.

On the other hand, a very musical person can find dancing performed to a familiar concerto or symphony too distracting. They maintain that the music was written to be heard, not danced. Choreographers and dancers also tend to alter the tempo, which can be irritating to a music lover. When Diaghilev first presented Manuel de Falla's *The Three Cornered Hat* in London, Ansermet was conducting at the tempo given to him by the composer, Massine was dancing at another and Diaghilev kept saying to the conductor 'You are too slow, my dear, you are too slow!'

Ideally ballet should be viewed without any preconceived ideas and just be accepted and enjoyed for the beauty of the movement.

Each year at Christmas ballet companies throughout the world present *The Nutcracker*, which is indeed a hardy annual in the ballet world. Adults accompanying children to this seasonal work have, as a result, been attracted to ballet. *Coppélia* is another ballet which has a great attraction for children as well as uninitiated adults. This is a ballet which is colourful with both national and classical dancing; the music presents no problems and is familiar. Both of these ballets benefit enormously from being played to children as their enthusiasm is contagious.

131

Ashton's ballet *La Fille Mal Gardée* is another work which is enjoyed by all ages. It has humour, spectacle, a type of pantomime Dame and plenty of action with delightful dancing. The French title might deter some, which is a great pity as it should not be missed. With the passage of time and the popularity of ballet for English speaking audiences, old classics such as *Casse Noisette* became *The Nutcracker* and *Lac des Cygnes* became *Swan Lake*. Statistics show that the classical ballets remain the most popular: *Swan Lake* and *The Sleeping Beauty* are always guaranteed to fill the house. The Tchaikovsky music is familiar and well loved and known to concert goers. Several concerts now have a danced excerpt as an additional item, which makes an introduction to a full ballet performance much easier.

Another excellent way to approach ballet is to choose a familiar story such as *Romeo and Juliet* or *The Taming of the Shrew*. These are perhaps more for adults, as children prefer swans, fairies and such like. The Bournonville classic *La Sylphide* with its Scottish setting and tartan kilts has a great visual appeal, together with some very fine dancing. This Romantic work has a strong feminine appeal.

Bournonville's ballet *Napoli* is possibly his most popular, with its setting in Naples and the background of Vesuvius. It is the type of ballet acceptable to all ages, full of dance, wedding festivities and an exhilarating finale which sends the audience away happy.

One of the most famous of ballets is *Giselle*. However, it does not enjoy the popularity of either *Swan Lake* or *The Sleeping Beauty* because the music is less familiar. It has a sad and haunting theme without a glittering palace scene and is therefore not so popular with children. It is a ballet which presents a great challenge to the ballerina: the second act shows the spirits (wilis) of young girls who have died before their wedding night and rise nightly from their graves to haunt any unfortunate man who comes their way. He is forced to dance until he dies. In spite of the morbidness, it is a ballet that should be seen, as it is not just for the connoisseur.

Ballet For All, a touring group attached to the Royal Ballet in London, has done much to introduce ballet to far-flung audiences. Founded in 1965 by Peter Brinson, it offered a repertoire which gave entertainment as well as instruction. Some of their most successful programmes showed how a dancer was trained and led into performances. Other programmes discussed ballets and their backgrounds. In 1979 the company was reconstructed and is now administered by the Royal Academy of Dancing.

Many countries have touring groups which visit schools and present

132

ballets on an educational level, although they do not possess the unique value of Ballet For All, which explained the ballets being given in a national repertoire.

It is not possible for everyone to see full-length classics but the smaller touring groups offer varied programmes of three or more short ballets. These are often an ideal introduction to the world of ballet as usually there is one dramatic work together with classical works.

In England, the Sadlers Wells Royal Ballet, the Scottish Ballet, Northern Dance Theatre and the New London Ballet are companies which have the repertoires of small works as well as the full-length classics. The Scottish Ballet dance *Giselle*, *Napoli* and *La Sylphide* as well as *Tales of Hoffman*, which is a story ballet with a great appeal. The Sadlers Wells Royal Ballet has a large and constantly changing repertoire, including *Coppélia*, *The Rake's Progress*, *Pineapple Poll*, *Les Rendezvous*, *The Prodigal Son* and *The Two Pigeons*.

In countries where the climate allows, there are open air performances of ballet given by national companies. Ballet presented in a Greek style theatre has a special enchantment and these performances always attract large audiences and are often an excellent introduction to ballet.

Unhappily, in England the weather does not permit open air performances but there are now programmes given in a large, specially designed tent, the Big Top. This houses a large audience and there is an informality and happy atmosphere as well as minimum prices. There is also a special appreciation of the work of the dancers which is not so apparent in a more conventional setting.

There are numerous contemporary dance companies and groups which offer dance programmes but it is advisable to check on these, as if one goes expecting to see pointe work and tutus it may prove to be startlingly different. Children who have learned modern dance at school will be used to contemporary movement as well as the music but to an older generation it can be far removed from what they look for in ballet.

The Ballet Rambert, originally a classical company, now only presents contemporary works, therefore the name of the company can be misleading. Contemporary dance is not necessarily the movements seen on a television screen or in shows. It offers some fine work and only by attending performances can one assess its value for oneself.

7
Modern Dance

Scepticism inevitably accompanies new ideas and innovations in the arts. Performances of new works in ballets, operas and music have frequently been hissed and booed, paintings have been withdrawn from exhibitions and writings suppressed. To step outside the conventions inevitably leads to opposition and only a strong dedication brings recognition, although this may not come until after the unfortunate artist has died.

Dance, in common with other arts, owes much to far sighted and inspired pioneers and it is through them that progress has been made. At the end of the nineteenth and beginning of the twentieth century, dance had little artistic merit and was not given serious consideration as an art form. A dancer's career lay with the ballets in music hall or in musical comedies and revues.

It was through the work of three American dancers, Maud Allan (1883–1956), Loie Fuller (1862–1928) and Isadora Duncan (1877–1927), that more serious consideration was brought to bear upon dance. These dancers were the first to express movement untrammelled by a classical ballet training. Using draped costumes and dancing bare-footed, they were not restricted by tight bodices and pointe shoes and introduced a freer dance form. Each of these artists made considerable contributions to dance.

Maud Allan was born in Canada but was brought up in the United States and always considered herself an American. It was during a visit to Italy that her interest in dance was aroused. She was inspired by the movement and flowing lines seen in the works of artists such as Leonardo da Vinci and Botticelli and endeavoured to convey these qualities in her dances. She also added distinction to her performances by using the music of Bach, Beethoven, Chopin, Mendelssohn and Schubert. She had studied music for many years and realised that the poor quality of music used for dancing was injurious to dance as an art. Although her dances were not great works of art they did much to raise the musical standard.

Isadora Duncan, the American pioneer of dancing who rebelled against the conventions of ballet. She established schools in Russia, France and America which did not survive her tragic death.

Loie Fuller's approach was rather different: she had spent many years in the theatre as an actress, singer and dancer and had a thoroughly professional outlook. In her dances she used yards of silken material which she manipulated skilfully and with great effect. She also used imaginative lighting which had not previously been seen and this technique was a closely guarded secret. Fuller was greatly admired and caught the spirit of the twenties and thirties. The Art Deco bronze and ivory figures which were then so popular were based on her dance compositions and have now become collector's pieces. Unlike Maud Allan, who toured constantly, Fuller worked mainly in France and was the first American dancer to be honoured in that country. Perhaps her greatest contribution was the use of stage lighting which now plays such an important part in modern theatre work.

Isadora Duncan came from San Francisco and was a flamboyant personality who looked to ancient Greece for her inspiration. Like Maud Allan she had an understanding of music and used the classics of Brahms, Chopin, Gluck, Beethoven and even Wagner. Music was the base of her interpretations and from it she created movement which expressed the themes and rhythmic structures of the composers. She was a highly individual artist and her performances aroused tremendous interest wherever she appeared. She toured extensively in Europe, the USA and especially in Russia.

All three artists appeared at a time when a new freedom was being expressed in art. Fokine was trying to develop these new ideas in his choreography at the Maryinsky Theatre and later with the Diaghilev Ballet. Duncan's choice of music impressed Fokine, for he felt that music was a major element of ballet and not just an accompaniment. In his choreography he never made the dancing subservient to the music. His inspiration, like Duncan's, came from the quality of the music and in Duncan he recognised similar ideals to his own.

The three protagonists of the new movement were all women and they worked in their individual ways to emancipate dance from the restrictions of the Victorian age. They tried to show that dance could be expressed in different ways.

Another American pioneer was Ruth St. Denis (1877–1968) who, like her fellow artists, made her name in Europe before achieving recognition in her own country. St. Denis turned to the East and Asia for her inspiration, taking ethnic themes and traditional steps and adapting them for stage use, the results being exotic and colourful. The East has always held a fascination for the peoples of Europe and oriental decoration and *objet d'art* were extremely popular at that time. Ruth St. Denis's company reflected this trend and her tours proved to be very successful.

Unhappily this was not the case in the USA where her company had many years of pioneer touring in vaudeville theatres which were then all that were available. In 1914 Ted Shawn (1891–1972), a young American dancer from Kansas City, joined the company and a year later, Shawn and St. Denis founded a school in Los Angeles called Denishawn. It was soon to become famous and from this cradle of American modern dance were to emerge many future dancers, teachers and choreographers. Shawn, during his years of touring with the company and later with his own company of male dancers, did much to destroy the prejudice against dancing for men.

In retrospect, this generation of dancers may not be considered very modern by today's standards but, to survive in the theatrical scene of that time, certain compromises had to be made. However, they were sincere in their beliefs and they introduced new aspects of dance to an interested public. They formulated ideas which were soon to develop and flourish.

Allan, Fuller and Duncan all founded schools but it was the next generation that was to produce the permanent form and technical basis which had been lacking in modern dance. Many of the principles of Duncan, Francois Delsarte (1811–71) and also of ethnic dance became incorporated into the new ideas.

The new innovators, Martha Graham (1894–   ), Doris Humphrey (1895–1958) and Charles Weidman (1901–75) were all from the Denishawn School and Company. They were each to explore an individual system of movement and devise a form that could be passed on to students. With a secure technique established, new choreographic ideas, could be expressed.

Graham was to evolve a technique based on the principles of contraction and release (the basis of breathing) with the concentration of movement in the solar plexus, together with the use of the spine and the back.

Humphrey and her partner Weidman had a very different approach based on the restoration of the body's balance following an off balance movement. This is referred to technically as fall and recovery. Both groups of dancers formed their own schools and established groups which presented their ideas. All were firm in their beliefs that modern dance should command its own merit and be accepted as a serious mode of expression. Subject matter was based on various aspects of the mind and emotions embracing the psychological ideas of Freud and Jung.

137

These themes had never been expressed in movement before and were far removed from those of conventional ballet. The costumes were severely cut, often full-length dresses without visual appeal for the girls, whilst the men wore working type trousers and shirts. In spite of hardships and misunderstandings, they persisted and slowly won a serious public for modern dance.

Graham gave her first concert, consisting of solos and trios, in 1926 and from then on has always maintained a company. Many of her finest choreographic works are still performed and the extensive tours carried out by the company are a tribute to her work. During the season at Covent Garden in 1979, fourteen of her ballets were performed including her latest work *The Owl and the Pussycat*, which featured the singer Liza Minnelli. Among her most notable ballets are *Appalachian Spring*, *Diversion of Angels*, *Seraphic Dialogue*, *Errand into the Maze*, *Cave of the Heart* and *Phaedra*.

Humphrey, in conjunction with her partner Weidman, formed a group which toured throughout the USA until 1940. Ill health forced its disbandment in the same year although she continued to choreograph and produced some of her best works for her protégé, Jose Limón (1908–72) and his company.

Parallel to the development of modern dance in America, a form of dance emerged in Germany during the early 1900s which became known as the Central European style of dance. This movement was indebted to a Frenchman, Francois Delsarte, who evolved basic laws and a scientific approach to the movement of the human body. It was known as *Applied Aesthetics* and was not confined to dance alone but extended to all movement. Several years later the Hungarian teacher and dancer Rudolf von Laban (1879–1958) developed and enlarged these ideas. Laban had a profound influence on dance in Germany and from his teaching emerged a style of dance very different from that of the Americans. All theories sought expressive freedom through the body but this attainment was sought through different approaches. Two of Laban's most influential pupils were Mary Wigman (1886–1973) and Kurt Jooss.

Wigman had been a Laban pupil for many years and had become his assistant before leaving to form her own school in Dresden. She gave performances throughout Germany, both as a solo artist and with her group of dancers, and the interest shown in her work enabled her to undertake a tour of the USA in 1930–31. This was the first visit to be made by a modern European company and reveals the development of interest in American modern dance. Mary Wigman's school trained some of the finest exponents of the new method of dancing and they spread the work both in Europe and the USA. Wigman's style was largely instrumental in establishing modern dance in Europe.

Laban's other brilliant pupil, Kurt Jooss, was, like Wigman, to leave and form his own school. In 1927 he became director of a school in Essen and three years later was appointed ballet master of the company at the Municipal Opera House in that city. In 1932 he took the company to Paris for the first choreographic competition of the Archives Internationales de la Danse, where they performed his ballet *The Green Table*. This ballet won first prize and established Jooss as a choreographer of note. Returning to Germany, he formed his own company, The Ballet Jooss, which toured extensively in the following years, and *The Green Table* became one of the company's most popular ballets. This work has been re-produced for many companies all over the world and it has remained the most successful of Jooss's works. Its theme is that of an assembly of arguing politicians and is still apposite today. Jooss used his style in a very theatrical way and his technical approach has stood the test of time, whereas the freer interpretations of Wigman are not seen today.

In Germany the Central European style of modern dancing became very firmly established and was dominant in the opera houses. It was also to have an influence on the other contemporary arts. In America, modern dance had to fight to win recognition, but in Germany it was popular to the point of excluding ballet. During the political upheavals a gradual decline took place, coinciding with the lack of brilliant pupils to develop the ideas of Mary Wigman. Only in America did her ideas continue to succeed.

Following a tour of the States, Hanya Holm (1898–　), one of Wigman's leading dancers and teachers, remained in New York and opened a school. The teaching of Holm combined with the stimulus and vitality of American dancers created a profound effect on modern dance. Together with Graham, Humphrey and Weidman, she became an outstanding figure in the modern dance world. In Germany, dance was accepted but in the States it was the driving force for recognition which kept it alive and as it declined in Germany, it flourished in the 'new country'.

From the struggle of the thirties and forties a new generation of dancers began to emerge; choreographers began to experiment and extend the range of movement in which they had been trained. Helped by ballet training, dancers began to move in a very different way. The old

139

idea that a dance composition should have a beginning and an end with a theme which was emotional or dramatic, was no longer followed. There was a completely different approach.

The Graham technique produced a formidable array of brilliant dancers and choreographers. Among them were Merce Cunningham, Erick Hawkins, Anna Sokolow, Paul Taylor and James Waring. One of the most outstanding was Merce Cunningham (1919–), whose creed was that dance should stand on its own and be completely independent of the musical accompaniment but, at the same time, the music and dance should be simultaneous entities. Music has also changed with the times, composers were experimenting and Cunningham was drawn to the works of John Cage (1912–). In 1942 a long association began between the composer and the choreographer. Cage composed numerous scores for Cunningham which incorporated electronic sounds, tapes and various noises.

Outstanding works of Cunningham, which have been re-produced by other companies, include *Summerspace*, *Rain Forest* and *Winterbranch*. His company has appeared all over the world and he has been a great influence on an avant-garde generation of dancers.

Paul Taylor (1930–) is a dancer and choreographer whose company has been seen on both sides of the Atlantic. It is classical in style and yet not balletic. His ballets show an unusual sense of humour, a feature so often lacking in modern dance programmes. Nureyev, who frequently appears with modern companies, has danced Taylor's ballet *Aureole*. Taylor's output covers over fifty ballets, including his well-known works *Three Epitaphs* and *Book of Beasts*.

A famous personality to emerge from the Humphrey–Weidman school was the Mexican, Jose Limón. His most outstanding work was *The Moor's Pavanne*, which is in the repertoire of many companies. Since his death his ballets, together with those of Humphrey, are preserved and performed by his dance group. It is important to view these works in perspective in the same way as those of Petipa and Fokine.

Alwin Nikolais (1912–) first studied dance after seeing Wigman on tour in the States. A pupil of Holm, he approached dance in a different way to that of his contemporaries. He possessed great versatility as not only was he a dancer but he also played the piano, composed, choreographed, taught and experimented with lighting. Not unlike Loie Fuller's conceptions, he evolved for his group, the Nikolais Dance Theatre, concepts of total theatre using dancers, props, lights, sound and colours, all playing equal parts in the production.

One of the first dancers to explore the possibilities of American themes was Helen Tamiris (1905–66). Trained in ballet, she developed her own individual approach, using, for the first time, Negro spirituals for many of her dance works. This idea was followed later by other choreographers.

Dance in the USA was not only confined to New York and the East coast but was growing in the West. In Los Angeles the dynamic Lester Horton (1906–53) formed a school and company and the latter was the first group to integrate various nationalities and races. His work was mainly in the West and not so well known in New York and the East. It was from this school that Alvin Ailey (1931–   ) was to emerge and form the Alvin Ailey American Dance Theatre. This company toured Europe on many occasions as well as the Far East, the USSR, Australia and Africa. His most famous ballets are *Blues Suite* and *Revelations*, but the company's repertoire includes ballets by Horton, Butler, Falco and Primus.

As dance companies became more widespread, Negro dancers began to form companies. Coloured choreographers absorbed ethnic, jazz and modern elements in the creation of a very personal and exciting dance form. Pearl Primus (1919–   ), Talley Beatty (whose very successful ballet *The Road of the Phoebe Snow* is in the repertoire of the Ailey company) and Katherine Dunham (1912–   ) all toured for many years in the USA and Europe. In the 1970s a new generation of dancers emerged, taking dance into further fields of experimentation often with strange and interesting results. The speed of present day living brings with it a quick exchange of ideas.

Companies and dancers known on both sides of the Atlantic include names such as: Murray Louis, Louis Falco, Remy Charlip, Philobolus Dance Theatre, Kei Takei, Meredith Monk, Lucinda Childs, Trisha Brown, Laura Dean and Twyla Tharp.

The works of Twyla Tharp receive much publicity and success. Her work *Push Comes to Shove*, created for the American Ballet Theatre, allowed Baryshnikov to give an astounding performance. Tharp was trained in Los Angeles and received a very comprehensive dance education, studying ballet, modern dance, jazz, tap and even baton twirling. Her choreography reveals her complete understanding of dance: she is able to link her movements with the culture of today. The music that she uses ranges from Fats Waller and Jelly Roll Morton to funk pop. This music presents no problems to the audience, unlike some contemporary scores, and this adds to her success and popularity.

Underlying much of her choreography is a seriousness combined with a sense of humour. Her work is also reminiscent of that seen in modern musicals, being highly inventive and original. Two of her more recent works for her company are *Baker's Dozen* and *Chapters and Verses*.

England has been more conservative in its outlook concerning changes within the arts. This has meant a slower acceptance of anything new in the contemporary scene.

Maud Allan had a great success in London prior to World War I although it was thought that her *Vision of Salome* was rather shocking. She had a great affection for London and returned during World War II to volunteer as an ambulance driver. She was one of the first to teach her form of movement in London.

Isadora Duncan had made people aware of the glories of ancient Greece and in the 1900s Ruby Ginner (1886–1978) devised a technique based on the classical poses found in Greek art. This form of movement, which had a strong technical basis, became very popular and is still taught and danced today. Others taking inspiration from classical Greece included Madge Atkinson (1885–1970), who took the natural line of the body as a foundation for the technique known as Natural Movement.

Margaret Morris (1891–1980), who had worked with Isadora's brother Raymond, also developed a similar system of dancing. The interest in the form of movement away from the classical technique became very evident. In these forms of movement the body lines were always well balanced and harmonious.

When Mary Wigman visited London for the first time, the angular Central European dance form was found hard to accept. One of the first to teach this style in England was Gertrud Bodenwieser (1886–1959), an Austrian dancer and teacher, and the interest she aroused was beginning to develop when the advent of World War II brought it to an end.

During the years of World War II, Kurt Jooss settled in England and presented some of his finest works. His company of excellent dancers did gallant work touring and it came as a surprise to many to find a company who danced in soft shoes and did not use pointe work or tutus. In 1951 Jooss returned to Germany and England was left without a modern company.

Martha Graham was a well-known name in Britain but few had seen her work or her company of dancers. In 1954 she brought to London for the first time some of her most famous works. The general public had not seen the Graham technique before: the music was modern and the décors by Isamu Noguchi (1904–) seemed strange. The reaction was such that the company must have felt that they were back to pioneering. When they returned in 1963 the pattern had changed as a more progressive attitude had been slowly developing. Modern Educational Dance, based on Laban's principles, was now part of the scholastic system. Through this and the modern trends there was a public interest which ensured a great success for the Graham company on its second visit.

English dancers who had been inspired by Graham, in the same way that Pavlova had been a source of inspiration in former years, now sought a training in the new dance form and it was through the patronage and far-sightedness of Robin Howard (1924–) that this became possible. Howard, a great admirer of Graham's work, arranged for several English dancers to go to New York to study in her studio. In 1965 classes were started in London and gradually a school became established which led to the forming of a company in 1967. The interest in the work increased and a permanent centre for both the school and company became an urgent necessity.

After a great deal of searching, a studio and theatre space was found at The Place. Since then the company, the London Contemporary Dance Theatre, has continued from strength to strength. In a very few years it has developed a style of its own and is now a company of very talented dancers and choreographers. The artistic director is Robert Cohan (1925–), an American dancer and choreographer, a pupil of Graham's as well as being her partner for eleven years. Associate choreographers are Micha Bergese, Siobhan Davies and Robert North, all of whom received their training at the London Contemporary Dance Theatre. They have made important contributions to the company's repertoire. The company tours extensively in England and overseas and one of their most successful tours was in the USA. This was the first time that a British-trained company had gained recognition in the home of modern dance.

The two major modern dance companies in England are now the Ballet Rambert and the London Contemporary Dance Theatre. The Ballet Rambert has several Tetley ballets in its repertoire, such as his much acclaimed *Pierrot Lunaire* and a full-length work, *The Tempest*. Siobhan Davies and Micha Bergese of the London Contemporary Dance Theatre have created works for them as well as the company's leading dancer Christopher Bruce (1945–), who has choreographed several

143

very successful ballets. The training of a modern dancer encourages choreographic talent and new ideas and ballets are constantly being shown, discussed and analysed. This seldom happens in the world of classical ballet.

Both the modern companies have schools and with the increased number of students interested in contemporary dance, smaller groups are emerging. Several of the new and small theatres now present dance programmes and groups also tour schools and art centres. Various universities and training colleges offer dance degrees which include modern dance in the curriculum.

The contemporary scene allows for interesting collaborations between students, artists, dancers, musicians and choreographers.

Touring groups usually consists of six or more dancers and although their existence is often threatened by economic factors, their convictions are sincere. The increasing interest being shown in the contemporary dance movement is demonstrated by the existence of such groups as the Emma Dance Company, Extemporary Dance Company, the Junction Dance Company, the Basic Space Dance Theatre, Richard Alston and Dancers, the Rosemary Butcher Dance Company, Maas Movers and The Cycles. A new following has grown which is separate from the audiences that support the classical ballet. The audience for contemporary dance has become more discerning and visiting companies face a critical attitude towards their work.

Ballet has also digressed into the modern field, as is reflected in the new works that appear. More choreographers work in a style which combines ballet technique and the use of pointe shoes, together with strong modern body lines. Both dance forms rely on each other, as ballet technique is used in the training of a contemporary dancer and modern techniques are becoming an essential part of classical training. MacMillan uses a very strong modern style, especially in his abstract ballets. Some choreographers, such as Tetley, have created ballets for both classical and modern companies. The very individual works of Twyla Tharp are performed both by classical dancers as well as by her own company and Merce Cunningham has choreographed a ballet for the Paris Opéra.

Modern dance has undoubtedly had an important influence on ballet and will continue to do so in the future. Dancers such as Makarova, Nureyev, Dowell, Seymour and Baryshnikov all excel in both modern and classical dancing. What of the future? Are these modern works just passing novelties? Does the ballet public really want to be dazzled by mixed media and stage effects? For many it is still the classical line which has the impact. The classical roles remain the greatest tests for a ballerina as Shakespeare's works remain the criterion for the actor. The realism of present day works is only an extension of the ideas of Noverre, Weaver and Hilverding. Speech and song as an accompaniment to dance is reminiscent of the court ballets of Louis XIV which integrated all the arts.

Shiva, the Lord of the Dance, is said to have created the world through dance, but equally his wild rhythms can destroy it at the end of the cosmic cycle—the future is in the lap of the gods.

Glossary

Adage   In class the word *adage* or *adagio* denotes a long sequence of exercises in slow tempo, either at the barre or in the centre, to develop the dancer's strength and the control of the legs and the back. In *pas de deux* the male dancer supports the ballerina as she performs *adage* movements on pointe.

Allegro   From the Italian, meaning lively and fast. In class it usually follows the *adage* and consists of jumping, beaten and turning steps.

Arabesque   A position in dancing in which the dancer stands on one leg, straight or bent, with the other leg extended to the back. There are various kinds of *arabesque* which are numbered according to the position of the arms. In an *arabesque allongée* the body is almost parallel with the floor and in an *arabesque penchée* the dancer leans forward and raises the leg higher, following the line of the body.

Assemblé   To assemble or bring together. A jumping step in which one leg brushes up and out either to the front, side or back whilst springing off the other. The feet are joined at the height of the spring before landing on both feet into a fifth position.

A terre   On or touching the ground.

Attitude   A position originally derived from Giovanni da Bologna's statue of Mercury, in which the dancer stands on one leg, bent or straight, with the other leg raised at the back or front in a bent position. In Soviet ballet the foot is raised higher than the knee but in Western training the knee is the highest point. The statue was said to have inspired the great teacher Carlo Blasis who introduced it into classical technique.

Auditorium   The part of the theatre in which the audience sits. The balcony, circle and stalls all form the auditorium.

Balancé   To swing or rock, a step which sways from side to side or in *battement balancé*, in which the leg is swung forwards or backwards.

Ballerina   A title given to the female dancer who performs leading roles. *Prima ballerina* means first dancer. In the USSR the title of *prima ballerina assoluta* has only been bestowed on three dancers: Pierina

Legnani, Mathilde Kschessinska and Maya Plisetskaya. In England this title was bestowed on Margot Fonteyn.

Ballet blanc   The name given to a ballet in which the female dancers are all dressed in white and portray sylphs, wilis, swans, etc.

Ballet Master or Mistress   Originally a person who was responsible for arranging and producing dances and ballets, either in a theatre or at court. They were also required to teach a company of dancers. An example is the Danish *Ballet Master*, August Bournonville; he formed a system of teaching and also choreographed numerous ballets.

Nowadays the title usually denotes a person who gives classes and rehearses the ballets which have been created by someone else. In Europe the name *Maître* or *Maîtresse de Ballet*, or *Balletmeister* or *Meisterin* is used and they are expected to choreograph part of the repertoire.

Ballon   A bouncing action: the quality is obtained by the smooth rise and fall of a dancer as he jumps and returns with a soft bending movement, or *demi-plié*. The term is often applied to leading male dancers or ballerinas who show this springing movement.

Barre   The wooden hand rail or bar which runs round the wall of a ballet studio at waist height. The dancer holds on to this during the first part of class. The term also refers to a work-out—a dancer will say 'I must do a *barre*'.

Batterie   A term referring to steps in which the feet or legs beat together or interweave in the air. A beat is frequently added to steps as an embellishment and to add brilliance. The word *battu* is sometimes used to denote a step which has an added beat.

Body tights   A tight-fitting all-over garment which is like a second skin and is made in cotton, nylon or Lycra. Body tights are frequently worn by modern dancers and have become the basic costume for many ballets.

Bourrée, pas de   A step in ballet which is derived from the folk dances of the Auvergne region in France. Many ballet steps have their origins in folk dance. There are twenty-six different ways of executing a *pas de bourrée*. Basically the weight is transferred from one foot to the other in three movements. *Pas de bourrée chaîne* or *couru* is a series of small even steps danced on pointe that gives the impression that the dancer is gliding across the stage. Pavlova was noted for her quick and beautifully executed *couru*.

Brisé, pas   Meaning a broken step, it consists of an *assemblé* embellished with a beat. In the final act of *The Sleeping Beauty* the male dancer performing in the Bluebird executes a series of *brise volé*, the beats occurring to the front and back. *Volé* is from the French *voler*, to fly, and the dancer gives this impression as he moves across the stage.

Cabriole   A jumping step, the name is derived from the Italian and means a caper. The dancer extends one leg to the front and, springing upwards, brings the second leg underneath it, causing the first leg to rebound a little higher before the dancer lands. The step is also executed to the side and back. Male dancers with a good elevation can execute double or triple *cabriole* : the legs beat together two or three times before landing. This step is frequently seen in male solos.

Character dancing   A character dancer is a person who specialises in the portrayal of a character through dancing and mime. Many famous dancers retired from more active roles bring their experience and knowledge to these roles and give considerable strength to the production. In the Royal Ballet, Gerd Larsen, Pamela May, Julia Farron, Leslie Edwards and Michael Somes all show great artistry in a variety of characters. Roles such as Carabosse in *Sleeping Beauty* are sometimes performed by leading ballerinas such as Lynn Seymour and Monica Mason. Character dancing can also refer to the national dances such as the mazurka or czárdás which occur in many of the classics. Drosselmeyer in *The Nutcracker* and Kastchey in *The Firebird* are other examples of character roles.

Choreographer   This is the name given to the composer or author of ballets. It comes from the Greek words *khoros*, to dance, and *graphein*, to write. It is the choreographer who invents the steps and shows them to his dancers. He devises the patterns and groupings, unfolds the story through movement and expresses the music through the dance steps. Prominent names in the choreographic world are Petipa, Fokine, Ashton, Balanchine and MacMillan.

Choreography   In the eighteenth century *choreography* only referred to the writing down of the steps of a dance, now known as dance notation. Today it is a term used for the actual arrangement of the steps in a finished work. Programmes will say, '*choreography* by . . .' and if the work is not successful then the choreographer is blamed. This is similar to the position of a playwright if a play is considered bad.

Coda   This is the final section of a *pas de deux*. In the famous *pas de deux* from *Don Quixote* the dancers first perform an adagio section and this is followed by a solo variation for each dancer. It then ends with a fast *coda* in which there is a brief solo for each performer before dancing the conclusion together.

Contemporary Dance   This is the term used by Martha Graham and others trained in this modern technique.

Corps de ballet   The name refers to the ensemble of dancers in a ballet company. In ballets such as *Les Sylphides*, *Swan Lake*, *Giselle* and *La Bayadère*, the sylphs, swans and wilis who are not soloists constitute the *corps de ballet*. Many dancers first begin in the *corps de ballet* and thus gain experience, strength and discipline prior to soloist status. The *London Evening Standard*, which gives annual awards for theatre performances, chose the Royal Ballet *corps de ballet* as the recipient of an award commending their exactness and perfection in the ballet *La Bayadère*. The term can also mean the company as a whole as are the dancers at the Paris Opéra.

Coryphée   This is the name given to a dancer who has moved out of the *corps de ballet* and who dances minor solo roles. In England the dancers are listed in programmes as Artists (which are the *corps de ballet*), then *Coryphées*, Solo Artists and Principals.

Danseur noble   A male dancer who performs in the noble classical style. The name comes from the seventeenth-century French court when Louis XIV appeared in ballets. When the king retired from dancing his roles were performed by professional dancers known as *danseurs noble*. The term has remained and is given to the interpreters of roles such as Prince Siegfried in *Swan Lake* and Albrecht in *Giselle*. Anthony Dowell is a fine example of a *danseur noble* because of his great dignity and bearing.

Demi-caractère   A style of dancing which has the form of a character dance but is executed with steps based on the classical technique. An example is Swanilda in *Coppélia*.

Demi-plié   A half bend of the knee and an essential movement as a preparation and conclusion of all jumping steps. The phrase 'more use of the *demi-plié*' frequently appears on examination reports and implies that the dancer performs with rather a stiff action in the knees.

Divertissement   This term refers to a series of dances which occur in a ballet as a form of entertainment. The fairy tale characters who appear in Act IV of *The Sleeping Beauty* form a *divertissement*. It can also mean a series of dances given in a ballet programme under this heading.

Double work   The technique of *pas de deux*, in which the male dancer gives support to the female dancer in her turns, lifts and balances. In large ballet schools classes are given in double work and sometimes the boys are given weight training exercises in preparation for lifting.

Elevation   The ability to jump high in the air. Nijinsky was noted for his elevation and the illusion of remaining suspended for a moment before landing. Baryshnikov has this same quality.

Enchaînement A series of steps linked together into a dance phrase, either in class or as part of a ballet. In dance examinations there are set *enchaînements* in the various syllabi and the candidates are also given *enchaînements* devised by the examiners.

Entrechat From the Italian, *intrecciare*, meaning to interweave. A jump in the air during which the legs pass quickly sideways, crossing and re-crossing, causing a beat of the calves. When the feet change twice it is called *entrechat quatre*, three times, *entrechat six*, four times, *entrechat huit* and (very rarely) five times, *entrechat dix*. Male dancers frequently perform this step as in the Bluebird solo variations, when a series of *entrechat six* are danced.

Epaulement Literally, shouldering. A term used to indicate the placing of the shoulders in relation to the body. Good *épaulement* can give a very expressive line to a movement or pose.

Fondu From the French, meaning melted. This is a smooth bending of the supporting knee whilst the other leg (the working leg) is either held in position or folds inwards or is extended. A good *fondu* action helps to give *ballon* and develops elevation.

Fouetté Meaning whipped, it is a turning step, usually done in a series in which the dancer whips the working leg out to the side and into the knee as a turn is made. It is performed by the ballerina on pointe. A famous series of thirty-two *fouettés* occurs in *Swan Lake*, Act III.

Foyer de la Danse At the Paris Opéra it was originally a retiring room at the back of the stage fitted with mirrors and bars. At one time it was popular with various patrons to watch dancers exercising before a ballet. It is now used for rehearsals and occasionally for certain productions. The Foyer can be opened on to the stage, giving it a tremendous depth. Many theatres are equipped with a Green Room which has the same purpose. Ashton choreographed a ballet for the Ballet Rambert in 1932 called *Foyer de Danse* : it was based on the Degas paintings of the famous Foyer.

Leotard A skin-tight garment like a one-piece swimsuit which is made with or without sleeves and has a variety of necklines and colours. It is used as a basis for some stage costumes and as a practice costume. The name is derived from Jules Leotard (1830–70), a famous French acrobat who was said to have invented the flying trapeze.

Mime In the *ballets d'action* of the eighteenth century the story was conveyed by gesture or mime. This custom of alternating mime and dance continued through the Romantic period and into the Petipa ballets and those of the late nineteenth century. A type of sign language was evolved which was devised from the *Commedia dell'Arte*. These conventional gestures may be seen in such ballets as *The Sleeping Beauty* when Carabosse curses the baby Aurora at the christening. *Giselle* has similar passages of mime with her mother and Albrecht. In more recent productions of the classics these passages are often omitted, abbreviated or replaced by dancing.

One of Fokine's reforms was to replace the conventional mime with the whole body expressing the action.

Mixed or Multi-media   Several choreographers have experimented by using different media to achieve an overall effect. Strobe or black lighting can highlight part of a costume which has been specially painted leaving the rest in the dark.

Simultaneous film, which reflects the movement of the dancer with the film image, is also used. Lighting and the use of slides, colour or a moving decor can all play a part in the conception of a ballet.

Alwin Nikolais and his dance company have evolved a very successful total theatre effect blending dancers, props, lights, sounds and colours, all of which play an equally important part in the whole production.

Modern Dance   This term covers a variety of different styles which range from jazz, technical systems of modern movement as opposed to classical training and educational dance.

Dance departments of universities and training colleges award dance degrees in which modern dance plays an important part. In England the term contemporary dance describes the movement derived from the Graham style. Modern dance is loosely used to cover all fields.

Notation   A system of writing and literally writing down movement. Notating movement dates back as far as the fifteenth century when letters were used as abbreviations for the well-known steps then in use. At that time the range of steps was limited so the notation was fairly simple. As dance steps developed, new systems of recording them were devised. It was Raoul Feuillet (1660–1710) who first invented a system using symbols although credit should go to Beauchamp who had originally devised it. Blasis, Bournonville and Saint-Léon all had their own methods.

In Russia at the Imperial Schools a system was used based on musical notes. This had been invented by Vladimir Stepanoff (1866–96) who recorded over thirty ballets in the Maryinsky repertoire. These manuscripts were consulted when the classic ballets were reproduced for the Vic-Wells Ballet in the early 1930s.

Today there are two major systems in use, choreology or Benesh notation and Labanotation or Kinetography Laban. The first system was invented by Rudolf Benesh (1916–75) and is used throughout the world. The Royal Ballet employs four Dance Notators or Choreologists.

Labanotation is also very widely used both for recording ballets or recording movement.

Pas   Meaning a step, the word is frequently used in ballet to describe steps such as *pas de chat*, *pas de bourrée* or *pas de basque*. It can also be used to mean dance, as in *pas de deux*, *pas de trois*, *pas de quatre*, meaning dances for two, three or four people.

Pas de deux   In a *pas de deux* the male dancer supports the ballerina and displays her to the best advantage. He shows her line, poise and balance. In modern *pas de deux* many of the lifts are very difficult and require great strength. The male partner has to avoid the look of any strain. He also has to judge the distribution of the ballerina's weight and be in complete sympathy with her movements. There is a great art in partnering which is often criticised by the critics.

Pirouette   This word refers to a turn in which the dancer spins on one leg with the other leg held below the knee, in arabesque attitude or out at the side (*à la seconde*). Male dancers can execute many turns on the spot without lowering the working leg. Female dancers, especially with a partner, can also perform several turns on pointe.

Placing   Essential in ballet is the correct placing of the body. The alignment of the head, neck, spine, hips and legs must all be controlled and balanced. The back should not be over-arched but the spine should be well extended. The pelvis should not be pushed forward or back and the shoulders must be aligned over the hips and the weight of the body evenly distributed on both feet. The correct stance has to be maintained throughout the execution of all the movements. The basic placing is frequently criticised on ballet report forms as it is of the greatest importance in the training of a dancer.

Plié   The word is from the French *plier*, to bend. It is an essential part of most dance movements. The exercise *plié* can be executed either *demi-pliés* (half bends) or *grands pliés* (full bends) and are the first movements practised by every dancer at the beginning of a class. Before a performance a dancer will warm up by a series of *pliés* in various positions.

Pointe   To dance on *pointe* is to dance on the tips of the toes in specially blocked shoes. It is not known exactly who was the first dancer to do this. The male dancers in the Caucasus have been famous for centuries for their dancing on the toes. For this they wear a soft leather boot.

In ballet it is the female dancers who train to dance on *pointe*, or on toe as it is called in some countries.

Male dancers rarely perform on *pointe* and it is only done to emphasise the comedy in a role. In Ashton's ballet *The Dream* the role of Bottom is highlighted by steps performed on *pointe*. Widow Simone (danced by a male) in *La Fille Mal Gardée* also dances amusing steps on *pointe* but in clogs, not pointe shoes.

Pointe shoes   The blocked shoes that are worn by dancers when dancing on their toes, or *sur les pointes*. Known in some countries as toe shoes, they are made of satin with a leather sole and a specially blocked or stiffened toe section. In the Romantic period, when dancing on the toes became a feature, the shoes were not blocked but were padded inside with cotton wool. In 1862 the shoes were stiffened with glue and the outsides darned for additional strength. Darning is still observed as it helps to prolong the life of the shoe. A ballerina will wear out a pair of shoes at a performance and will need a new pair for each act of a full-length ballet. France and Italy were the centres for the manufacture of ballet shoes but it has now become universal. Larger ballet shoe manufacturers make over 1,700 pairs of shoes a day, which is an indication of the popularity of ballet.

Port de bras   This term, from the French, means the carriage of the arms. In ballet the whole of the body is trained and the use of the arms is as important as footwork. A series of exercises are performed to develop a flow and quality to arm movements. Dancers are criticised for their lack of breadth and tenseness in their *port de bras*.

Carlo Blasis said that 'when the arms accompany each movement of the body with exactitude they may be compared with the frame that sets off a picture. If the frame is so constructed as not to suit the picture, however well executed the latter may be, the whole effect is unquestionably destroyed'.

Positions   There are five basic positions of the feet, first codified by the French dancing master, Beauchamp, in the seventeenth century. They are still used today and are the basis of most classical ballet steps.

In the *First Position* the heels are touching and the feet fully turned out in a straight line.

In the *Second Position* the feet are placed apart in a straight line, the distance between the heels being approximately one and a half lengths of the dancer's feet.

The *Third Position* has one foot in front of the other with the heel against the instep.

In the *Fourth Position* the feet can be placed in two ways: (a) one foot in front of the other opposite the first position and called *ouverte* or open, (b) opposite the fifth position, *croisé* or crossed.

The *Fifth Position* has one foot in front of the other with the heel of each foot against the joint of the big toe of the other foot.

The first, third and fifth are closed positions and the second and fourth are open. The numbers of second and fourth are also used when the foot is pointed forward, back or at the side, either *à terre* or *en l'air*.

The arms also have set positions but these vary according to the system being taught.

Rake   Many theatres have a sloping or raked stage which means that the stage is built higher at the back and gradually slants downwards to the footlights. In older theatres the rake can be quite steep. The purpose of the rake was to enable those sitting in the stalls to have a better view of the performers. Most modern theatres are now built with a flat stage and the seats in the auditorium are raised. Dancers experience difficulty performing on a raked stage and many opera houses have a rehearsal room which has a raked floor similar to that of the stage.

Romantic Ballet   The period of the Romantic era was approximately from 1830 to 1850 and it was in this period that the ballerina became prominent. During this time the ballets reflected the ideals of the Romantic movement and were danced in exotic settings with the ballerina's portrayal of the artist's dream of the unattainable. *La Sylphide* and *Giselle* are two examples of the ballet of the period.

The Romantic style and mood was used by Fokine in 1909 when his ballet *Les Sylphides* was presented in Paris by the Diaghilev Ballet Russe and danced by Pavlova, Karsavina and Nijinsky. The tutu and classical hair style of the Romantic period is still worn for this ballet.

Rosin   Made from crude turpentine, rosin looks like small rocks or stones and is easily crushed into a powder. It is used on dancers' shoes to prevent slipping. A tray of rosin is kept in the studio or wings so that the soles of the shoes can be rubbed into it. Highly polished stage surfaces can be very dangerous for dancers.

Stage directions   Various terms are used in stage directions. Up stage means moving away from the footlights and down stage means moving towards them. Cecchetti adopted numbers, facing the audience was five, the right hand corner was one, the left hand corner two, left corner

154

back three, etc.

Tights The stocking type garment which covers a dancer from the waist to the feet. They are said to have been invented by Maillot, a costumier at the Paris Opéra in the nineteenth century, and in French the word *maillot* means tights. It is probable that a form of stocking was worn before this date. With the use of net and shorter skirts they became extended into tights. They are now bought in various colours with or without feet. For class and practice woollen tights are frequently used but many prefer to use woollen leg warmers over nylon tights.

Tour en l'air This is a step in which the dancer jumps straight upwards and makes a turn in the air before landing. Usually performed by men who execute two turns or double *tours en l'air*. A dancer with a high elevation can turn three times but a double turn is the most usual. This occurs in many male solos and in *Giselle*, Act II, Albrecht dances a series of them.

Travesti, en In the second half of the nineteenth century the position of the male dancer had declined so much that he was termed *porteur*: his only function was to support and carry the ballerina. Many of the male roles were danced by females in male costume, a practice common in most opera houses. Adeline Genée was frequently partnered by an *en travesti* dancer at the Empire Theatre in London.

In Russia *en travesti* dancers were not used and it was only with the advent of the Diaghilev ballet into Europe that the male dancer regained recognition.

In some ballets the roles of women were taken by men, for example, the Ugly Sisters in *Cinderella*, Widow Simone in *La Fille Mal Gardée* and the Headmistress in *Graduation Ball*. All of these roles are in the pantomime tradition of an old theatrical origin.

Turn-out In the seventeenth, eighteenth and into the nineteenth century it was thought that to walk with slightly turned out feet was very fashionable. It first developed about 1620 at the French Court, then the centre of European fashion, and was copied by the rest of Western Europe. The court dances at this time also changed and the French Baroque technique required the use of turn-out. Louis XIV, the Sun King, excelled at a dance called Slow Courante which firmly established the turn-out of legs and feet. The professional dancers, when taking over the court ballets on Louis's retirement, had no difficulty in turning out. Trained as acrobats, they had a pliability which they were soon to develop. Gradually the turn-out became established by Blasis in a 90 degree position. This has been used ever since and to achieve the turn-out of the leg in the hip socket takes a long time and can only be obtained through continual exercises. It was popular at one time to try and force a turn-out by placing a dancer's feet into a *tourne hanche*. This was a round box-like instrument into which the feet were strapped. The dancer would remain imprisoned in it for half an hour or more.

Tutu   The name given to the ballet skirt worn by dancers. The calf-length tarlatan skirt worn by Taglioni in *La Sylphide* became the pattern for the *tutu* of the ballerina. The skirt became shortened as ballerinas acquired greater virtuosity. From just above the knee it gradually developed into the short classical *tutu* of the present style, in which the net projects straight out at hip level. It is not easy to make as the tarlatan skirt is fixed to a tight fitting basque joined to the low-cut bodice.

Variation   A solo dance. In the Petipa ballets the prima ballerina always performed one or more variations to display her technique. The fairies in *The Sleeping Beauty* all perform a variation each.

Warm-up   Before a rehearsal or performance a dancer will prepare the muscles with a series of exercises. They are usually barre exercises combined with various stretching movements. Woollen leg warmers, which are like thick stockings without feet, are worn to keep the muscles pliable. Rehearsals sometimes involve a great deal of waiting about and it is essential to keep the body warm and avoid any strain. Back stage in theatres can also be very draughty and leg warmers help to give protection. It has been known for a dancer to forget to take them off and appear on stage wearing them!

Recommended Reading

Austin, Richard (1978) *Natalia Makarova*, Dance Books.

Bland, Alexander (1978) *A History of Ballet and Dance*, Barrie & Jenkins.

Bland, Alexander (1976) *The Nureyev Image*, Studio Vista.

Blasis, Carlo (1968) *An Elementary Treatise upon the Theory and Practice of the Art of Dancing*, Dover Publications.

Brinson, Peter and Crisp, Clement (1970) *Ballet For All*, Pan.

Buckle, Richard (1971) *Nijinsky*, Weidenfeld & Nicolson.

Buckle, Richard (1979) *Diaghilev*, Weidenfeld & Nicolson.

Clarke, Mary and Crisp, Clement (1978) *Ballet in Art*, Ash & Grant.

Clarke, Mary and Crisp, Clement (1978) *Design for Ballet*, Studio Vista.

Clarke, Mary and Vaughan, David (1977) *The Encyclopedia of Dance and Ballet*, Pitman.

Clarke, Mary and Crisp, Clement (1976) *Introducing Ballet*, Studio Vista.

Crisp, Clement (1973) *Ballet: An Illustrated History*, A & C Black.

Crisp, Clement (1974) *Making a Ballet*, Studio Vista.

Croce, Arlene (1978) *Afterimages*, A & C Black.

Demidov, Alexander (1978) *The Russian Ballet Past and Present*, A & C Black.

de Valois, Ninette (1978) *Step by Step*, W H Allen.

de Valois, Ninette (1937) *Invitation to the Ballet*, John Lane.

Dolin, Anton (1953) *Markova, Her Life and Art*, W H Allen.

Duncan, Isadora (1966) *My Life*, Gollancz.

Fonteyn, Margot (1975) *Autobiography*, W H Allen.

Fonteyn, Margot (1979) *The Magic of Dance*, BBC Publications.

Glasstone, Richard (1977) *Better Ballet*, Kaye & Ward.

Guest, Ivor (1970) *Fanny Elssler*, A & C Black.

Guest, Ivor (1974) *Fanny Cerrito*, Dance Books.

Guest, Ivor (1972) *The Romantic Ballet in England*, Pitman.

Guest, Ivor (1979) *The Romantic Ballet in Paris*, Dance Books.

Haskell, Arnold (1977) *Balletomania*, Weidenfeld & Nicolson.

Kersley, Leo and Sinclair, Janet (1973) *A Dictionary of Ballet Terms*, A & C Black.

157

Kerensky, Oleg (1973) *Anna Pavlova*, Hamish Hamilton.

Kirstein, Lincoln (1975) *Nijinsky Dancing*, Thames & Hudson.

Kirstein, Lincoln (1979) *Thirty Years: The New York City Ballet*, A & C Black.

Koegler, Horst (1979) *The Concise Oxford Dictionary of Ballet*, Oxford Univ. Press.

Krementz, Jill (1979) *A Very Young Dancer*, A & C Black.

Lawson, Joan (1978) *Ballet Stories*, Ward Lock.

Lawson, Joan (1977) *The Story of Ballet*, Ward Lock.

Lawson, Joan (1973) *An History of Ballet and its Makers*, Dance Books.

Lawson, Joan (1977) *Beginning Ballet*, A & C Black.

Levinson, André (1977) *Marie Taglioni*, Dance Books.

Mackie, Joyce (1973) *Basic Ballet*, W Russell Turner.

McDonagh, Don (1976) *The Complete Guide to Modern Dance*, Doubleday.

McDonagh, Don (1973) *Martha Graham*, David & Charles.

Mazo, Joseph (1979) *Prime Movers*, A & C Black.

Monohan, James (1976) *The Nature of Ballet*, Pitman.

Payne, Charles (1979) *American Ballet Theatre*, A & C Black.

Percival, John (1975) *Nureyev*, Faber & Faber.

Roslavleva, Natalia (1966) *Era of the Russian Ballet*, Gollancz.

Salter, Elizabeth (1978) *Helpmann*, Angus.

Sorrell, Walter (1969) *Hanya Holm*, Wesleyan Univ. Press.

Spatt, Leslie (1978) *Stuttgart Ballet*, Dance Books.

Streatfield, Noel (1978) *A Young Person's Guide to Ballet*, Warne.

Swope, Martha (1979) *Baryshnikov at Work*, A & C Black.

Taper, Bernard (1964) *Balanchine*, Collins.

Vaughan, David (1978) *Frederick Ashton*, A & C Black.

Verdy, Violette (1977) *Giselle*, Dekker.

Wilson, G B L (1974) *A Dictionary of Ballet*, A & C Black.

Winter, M Hannah (1974) *The Pre-Romantic Ballet*, Pitman.

Bibliography

Blasis, Carlo (1968) *An Elementary Treatise upon the Theory and Practice of the Art of Dancing*, Dover Publications.

Brahms, Caryl (1943) *Robert Helpmann*, Batsford.

Bruhn, Erik and Moore, Lilian (1961) *Bournonville and Ballet Technique*, A & C Black.

Buckle, Richard (1971) *Nijinsky*, Weidenfeld & Nicolson.

Clarke, Mary and Vaughan, David (1977) *The Encyclopedia of Dance and Ballet*, Pitman.

Guest, Ivor (1965) *A Gallery of Romantic Ballet*, New Mercury.

Lifar, Serge (1954) *A History of Russian Ballet*, Hutchinson.

McDonagh, Don (1976) *The Complete Guide to Modern Dance*, Doubleday.

Quirey, Belinda (1976) *May I Have the Pleasure*, BBC Publications.

Sitwell, Sacheverell (1948) *The Romantic Ballet*, Batsford.

Wilson, G B L (1974) *A Dictionary of Ballet*, A & C Black.

Winter, Marian Hannah (1974) *The Pre-Romantic Ballet*, Pitman.

Wosier, Maria-Gabriele (1974) *Sacred Dance*, Avon.

Index

The figures in **bold** refer to colour plates. Those in italics refer to the page numbers of black and white illustrations. Other figures refer to text pages.